*Speech in the
Elementary Classroom*

# Speech in the Elementary Classroom

By **CHARLES VAN RIPER**

and **KATHARINE G. BUTLER**

*Harper & Row, Publishers*
*New York, Evanston, and London*

SPEECH IN THE ELEMENTARY CLASSROOM

Library of Congress catalog card number: 55-10943

# Contents

73277

# Contents

# *Preface*

🦋 MANY classroom teachers, or students preparing to be teachers, have been disappointed after enrolling in the course commonly labeled "Speech for the Classroom Teacher." We have met many who have felt cheated when they found it to be merely another course in fundamentals of speech or public speaking. "I know my own speech could stand some improvement," they say, "but what I really need even more are some techniques and methods for improving the speech of my children. The whole structure of modern education is oriented toward pupil participation, and this means an immense amount of oral communication. But my children find it very difficult to express themselves orally. They speak very poorly as far as pronunciation and voice are concerned. Their fluency in reciting, in verbalizing their insights and observations is sadly broken. They find it difficult to express their real meanings. Much of my time is spent in interpreting what they have to say, in guessing what they are trying so hard to communicate, in translating to the other members of the class the true content of what they are uttering so confusedly. I think our schools have failed our children more in this than in any other vital skill. The adults who come out of our public schools are afraid to talk in public and with good reason. Give me something for my children! Much as I need help myself, I also need training so that I will not perpetuate the inadequacies I have known."

This book is expressly designed to serve such a teacher or prospective teacher. There are many texts centering about the improvement of the teacher's speech but few, if any, devoted to the child's oral communication. We have here concentrated on the area of the elementary school because it is there that the basic skills are formed and the poor habits stabilized. The increasing emphasis upon communication skills in the college years is evidence of the woeful lack of it on the elementary level. Our present culture is a highly verbal one. If we are to prepare our children to participate effectively in it, we must not neglect this most important phase.

While we have designed this text primarily to help the elementary teacher, we have found the materials within it to have important value for the public-school speech therapist. Many times the latter is given the task of introducing a speech program into a new school system or of helping the classroom teachers with their special problems. A good speech improvement program is of inestimable aid to the public-school speech therapist. It reduces her case load. It solves many of the difficulties in getting a child to carry over his newly acquired speech skills into his normal communication. It takes care of many emotional problems. In the interests of their own efficiency, many public-school speech therapists have voluntarily instituted a speech improvement program.

In the course of her teaching experience, every classroom teacher will meet a good many children with obvious speech defects. And usually she will not know what to do with them. In those school systems where a speech correction teacher's services are available, there is still need for the help of the classroom teacher in consolidating the newly taught speech sounds, the more adequate voice, or the improved fluency. A well-meaning but ill-informed classroom teacher can hurt these children more than the speech correction teacher can help them.

Moreover, there are still many school systems where no professional speech therapy services are provided. Whether she wishes to do speech correction or not with the children in her charge, the elementary teacher is faced with an important challenge. The child whose articulation is woefully defective will often find reading and spelling incredibly difficult. Such a child is also the cause of many problems in discipline because of his frustration. The child with a cleft palate or or peculiar voice can likewise be a thorn in the teacher's side. The boy who stutters can break up a class recitation or put a damper on all spontaneity. Or, without any reason, the parents may blame the teacher because it was during her classes that his speech defect became much more severe. Every teacher needs certain information about the disorders of speech. We have tried to provide it here.

But the basic aim and function of this book is to give the classroom teacher the tools she needs to help not just the speech-defective children but all her pupils. Oral communication is so important in our lives that it must no longer be neglected in our elementary schools.

C. Van Riper
K. Butler

*July, 1955*

# 1
## The Need for Training
## in Oral Communication Skills

❧ EVERY elementary teacher has had to face the problem of helping her children communicate more effectively. Indeed, her very livelihood depends upon her skill in accomplishing this, for teaching is as much the receiving as it is the sending of messages. The successful teacher must constantly know how her pupils are reacting to the stimulation she is providing. In part, this information comes from the silent language of postures, gestures, and facial expressions, and a good teacher is remarkably adept at translating these signs. But there is no form of communication so flexible or all-revealing as the child's speech. Anyone who has ever tried to teach a group of silent, repressed pupils knows how difficult and depressing the task can become. On the other hand, when children are all galvanized into swift give-and-take communication and the ideas and feelings are being exchanged with complete and mutual understanding, teaching becomes a wonderful profession.

Without thinking much about it, we tend to assume that the ability to express ourselves adequately and easily develops spontaneously in the child. We think of children who possess skills in communication as possessing special gifts. In our language, we speak of the "gift of gab." But these are not in-born traits; they are skills. They are the product of a learning process. True, much of this learning is not the result of deliberate teaching on the part of parents or teachers, but certainly we cannot reserve the term *learning* for the product of pedagogy alone. A few of our children have learned their techniques of oral communication fairly well; the great majority have not. Shall we then place all responsibility for such learning on the child? Or shall we do all we can to help him acquire facility in expressing himself—a facility which our society so highly rewards both in school and in later life?

**SPEECH IMPROVEMENT**

The school's effort to improve oral communication is usually labeled "speech improvement." We shall use this term for reasons of brevity, but we wish to make clear that by it we mean much more than most people do. We do not restrict this training to the improvement of pronunciation or grammar, nor do we use "speech improvement," as some other texts have, to designate a program of oral interpretation, public speaking, elocution, or debate, diluting and transposing courses in these subjects into unreasonable facsimiles suitable for children. One of the reasons why elementary schools have resisted any curriculum revision to include training in oral communication is that the type of "speech improvement" which is often suggested is based upon these college speech courses. No matter how skillfully they are reworked "for children," such activities are simply not suitable for them. We must evolve a program based on the type of communication children actually use.

Speech improvement, as we will treat the subject, is more

than tongue exercises, memorization, vocal phonics, articulation drills, and activities. It is more than instruction in the improvement of voice quality, pitch, and intensity. It is more than training in the ebb and flow of speech rhythms. Indeed, it is more than the sum total of all these parts. Speech improvement should go far beyond the mechanics of speech drills into the area of meaningful language. One of the most important aims might well be to help the children to verbalize their thoughts—to be able to "think on their feet" efficiently and adequately.

Many an adult would envy this kind of training. The inability to express ourselves clearly and appropriately often results in shunning positions of leadership or even equality within our social or business circles. We prefer anonymity to the torture of a pounding heart, perspiring hands, butterflies in our stomach, a tongue that cleaves to the roof of our mouth, and a mind seemingly frozen in fear. So we sit silently by, and then, when the opportunity has passed, we berate ourselves for our lack of initiative. We envy those more fortunate speakers who possess an agile tongue but we do not attempt to compete with them.

## THE NEED FOR SPEECH IMPROVEMENT

The need to express ourselves adequately is of paramount importance in this most vocal of worlds. The strong, silent individual might have made an excellent caveman, but even the rare cavemen of today need to be anything but silent. Psychologists have shown that we win and lose jobs, not on how little or how much we know, but rather on how well we are able to "sell" ourselves and our talents. The ability to think aloud has become an economic necessity.

Children, too, are likely to feel inadequate in their oral communication. From babyhood on, they are able to comprehend speech which they are unable to imitate successfully. Not only does the small child lack the vocabulary for full expression of his own desires, but also he finds that through speech adults try to make him conform to adult standards. The adult feels as free to turn off the child's speech as he does to turn off a faucet. "Please be quiet!" is merely a more polite version of "Shut up!" and all children know the admonition well. That the adult rarely succeeds in his attempt can be seen in the behavior of the child. He continues to "drip" speech, just as a leaky faucet puts forth a continuous spatter. This is not rank disobedience, as it might appear at first glance. Rather, the child's inner thinking and mental imagery are so closely associated with the vocal expression that he finds it difficult to separate them. Adults might remember that "thinking out loud" on a difficult problem is an aid in resolving that problem and they often do it themselves. The child has not learned to dissociate inner and outer thinking at the high level which the adult has reached. And even at this high level, adults are prone to say, "Let's talk this thing out!"

Speech improvement, therefore, should be taught in such a manner that it helps the child attain a level of speech competence sufficient to satisfy his psychological as well as his physical needs for emotional release.

## THE RESPONSIBILITY FOR IMPROVED SKILLS IN ORAL COMMUNICATION

During the past few years there has been an ever widening movement in educational circles to have the classroom teacher do much of the instruction in speech improvement. It is being realized that speech improvement practices and procedures should not be the sole property of the speech teacher or the speech correctionist in the public schools. All children will benefit from some phase of speech improvement, and it is the classroom teacher who is acutely aware of the need for this type of instruction. She recognizes the indistinct, hesitant speech of the shy child; the rather halting, stumbling speech of the poorly coördinated child; the loud, strained tones of the aggressive child. None of these children is "speech defective" in the sense that his speech is beyond the normal range; none of these children will receive help from the speech therapist even if such a specialist is employed by the school system. The speech therapist recognizes the need for helping these so-called "fringe children," but under most state regulations her case load prevents her from spending any time with the "normal" child. She must spend her few hours with those children presenting the clinical picture of marked speech abnormality and her time is already much too limited.

In view of these facts it is interesting that in many school systems the speech correction teacher has voluntarily instituted programs of general speech improvement in the early grades. She has done this usually for selfish reasons. Her case load is so large that, to allow enough time for the severe cases, she has taken on the additional task of speech improvement classes. She does so in order to free herself from the demands of many of the milder cases with whom she would otherwise have to work individually. Moreover, she has often found that these children are usually to be viewed as normal children whose speech skills have been maturing slowly. They can hardly be considered bona-fide speech defectives. Many of them seem to learn much better from their fellow classmates than from an adult. So the speech correction teacher, often reluctantly, teaches classes in speech improvement to all the children in the kindergarten, first grade, or second grade.

Appalled by the verbal inadequacies of high-school students, the administrators of a school system sometimes take the initiative for organizing a program of speech improvement in the elementary grades. Teachers have been exhorted to stress the improvement of "oral English" in every subject and activity, and certain periods are set aside for this purpose. However, the results of these programs have hardly been in keeping with their aims, primarily because the classroom teachers do not know what to do. They attempt to correct errors in pronunciation and to provide opportunities for class discussion or plays, but their children pass from grade to grade and out of the high school's commencement door still nonfluent, still fearful of formal speech, still with poor voices and sloppy articulation, still unable to express themselves with clarity. To provide the classroom teacher with a set of high-sounding goals and aims is hardly equivalent to providing her with the techniques for achieving them. Every teacher feels the pressure to help her children talk better but few of them know what to do. Most of them do a little and let it go at that. A few request the services of the public-school speech correctionist or the high-school speech teacher. The latter's training has been in the more formal types of speech and she, though willing, seldom can help very much. The speech correction teacher often is willing to put on demonstration lessons or even to carry on a yearly program of speech improvement in the classroom. At best, however, this is but a stopgap and can hardly be said to provide sufficient aid. Besides, the speech correction teacher tends to stress "corrective" factors too much and to slight training in efficient oral communication. Her own training makes her prone to work with errors rather than communication.

And so the basic responsibility remains with the classroom teacher.

## HOW THE CLASSROOM TEACHER HAS TRIED TO IMPROVE ORAL COMMUNICATION

During this century great changes have occurred in classroom activities. There is no better evidence of the teachers' gallant response to a real need of their children than the contrast between a schoolroom of seventy years ago and one of today.

The country school of that time was likely to be a dilapidated structure, warmed by a temperamental iron beast of a stove which often resisted the efforts of the schoolmaster to coax enough heat to thin the ink. Schoolmasters of the early days ruled by long beech switches which hung on hooks against the wall. Although punishment was likely to be rapid and severe, the boys in the class were always happy to risk it, if only to escape boredom. It was an exciting sport, like bullbaiting, or poking sticks through a fence at an angry dog. It was reported by one schoolmaster that "deeper observations of life and of human nature convinced him that the ministry of pain was God's great means of developing strength and

Education in Great-Grandfather's Day.

elevation of character; and that children should early understand this, that they might accept it as a moral blessing."[1] He therefore laid on the rod with a right good will.

Silence was golden in the schoolroom of our grandfathers, to be broken only by those who were "called up" to recite their history, geography, grammar, and reading. Young chil-

[1] Elizabeth Peabody, *Record of Mr. Alcott's School, Exemplifying the Principles and Methods of Moral Culture*. Boston: Roberts Brothers, 1874, p. 33.

dren were required to go through Webster's spelling book anywhere from five to ten times before they were considered fit to begin to read.

By 1870 many a schoolmaster had been replaced by a feminine counterpart, a young woman chosen from among the unmarried women in the home neighborhood. Many things remained the same—the drinking pail, the ferrule and switch, the prized rear seats, which were occupied by the oldest and the largest of the children. While these seats were undoubtedly the coldest in the school, this was more than compensated for by the fact that they were also farthest from the teacher. But teachers changed, as can be seen by the "Confessions of a Bad Boy who Reformed":

> I was a cureious little boy when I first went to school. I dident like to go anyway. I would torment the teacher the wordst kind and I would do every thing that she dident want me to do and if she wanted me to do a thing I wouldent do it and she got so mad with me she would shut me up in the closit but that dident do no good. I would get out of the window and go home. when I got up to read I would say whatever came into my mind and she would send me to my seat. and I would sit and laugh over it like a monkey but she thought she would try a new rule to be sure. she would give me a good whipping with the ruler when I dident mind. that I got use to after a while and dident mind it when I came to school in the winter I would bring snow in on my feat    she would tell me to go back out. I was so cold I dident want to and she would give me a good shaking and I liked it beaucause it warmed me up. the next teacher we got was better than the first one    she I liked very much. . . .[2]

Teachers and teaching have changed, indeed, since the turn of the century. Schoolrooms now are filled with all man-

[2] Clifton Johnson, *The Country School.* New York: Thomas Corwell and Company, 1907, p. 158.

ner of things. Gardens are grown; animals are cared for and studied; toys are played with; books are supplied with colorful pictures; and children are allowed to smile, to laugh, and most important of all, to *talk*.

There is a pleasant hum about a busy classroom where the teacher and her pupils are studying and learning together. The room is cheerful with plants and pictures; it is well lighted and heated. But pedagogy has discovered that learning can also take place outside a classroom, and so if the outside world cannot be brought into the school, the school goes out to explore the world.

The modern school is not silent. It talks; it sings; it shouts. It discovers and learns through the medium of speech. In the first and second decades of this century, teachers began to realize the need for training in speech. In 1915 the first "Speech Improvement Week" was held. And as teachers noted the existence of many speech impediments, and recognized the need for helping their children with speech difficulties, a variety of professional organizations was formed among teachers. Among these were the National Association of Academic Teachers of Public Speaking, the National Council of Teachers of English, the American Association for the Study of Speech Disorders, and finally, much later, the American Speech and Hearing Association.

Following, and paralleling, the growth of speech therapy provisions for the speech-defective child has come a growing realization of the equally important need for instruction for the normal child.

As the rigid and formalized manner of instruction in subject matter has given way to a more informal approach, so has the "speaking of pieces" evolved into a much more nor-

Education Today.

mal and basic approach to the teaching of speech skills. This change has come hand in hand with the widening of the public school's curriculum to include something more than the traditional three R's. As the school's activities have grown, and as the teacher has come to concern herself with more and more areas of her pupils' lives, emphasis has shifted from a mere Chinese memorization of academic material to a real effort to establish a communicative basis for living and learning. Both of these require a great amount of speech.

# II
# *Teaching and Talking*

❦ IN THE classroom of today most learning takes place through oral communication. Much of the academic material is presented orally by the teacher. Books, maps, pictures, films serve as guides and supplementary material, but most of the burden is still the teacher's, as many a raw throat at the end of a hard teaching day will testify. She recognizes that oral communication can be the most interesting, the most stimulating, and the most rewarding of all teaching methods. She also knows that true understanding is often a reciprocal affair. It is, in essence, an exchange of ideas and this exchange is a verbal one. Pupil as well as teacher must be able to express himself and his ideas if this understanding is to occur. To receive informative messages is not enough. He must be able to send them as well. How else can either teacher or pupil judge his accomplishments? Good teachers have long recognized this need and have attempted to devise various methods for giving children an *opportunity* to develop and use communicative skills.

### SHARING TIME

"Telling time" or "sharing time" has come to be considered standard procedure in most early elementary classrooms.

Sharing time is usually employed by the teacher at the beginning of the morning or afternoon session and is used as a transitional as well as a release device. The children troop into the room with the glow of outdoor freedom still upon them. Sharing time calms them down. It becomes a transition period for transferring interest from play activities to work activities, from self-absorption to listening attentively to others.

Sharing time gives each child the opportunity to present or relate that which is most important, not only to the teacher, but to the rest of the class as well. A new doll may be shown by a kindergartner; the death of a family pet is related with sorrow by a second-grader; a trip to a museum is described by a sixth-grader. Wise teachers use such opportunities to draw out the shy and retiring child; to give the aggressive child a chance to speak with authority; to encourage the withdrawn child to participate. For the child who is momentarily glorified by standing in front of a group of his peers and relating an incident or showing an object, it is an opportunity to speak, to be superior, to be in command (for the moment, at least), and to be, in essence, "the teacher." For the rest of the group, sharing time means listening intelligently and quietly if anything is to be gained from this activity. If the child standing before the group speaks well, the others will listen; if he mumbles, hesitates, wanders down verbal byways or dead-end streets, the group soon loses interest and ceases to listen. Good speech is indirectly rewarded through the group's attention; poor speech is also similarly penalized. The teacher, although in the verbal background, directs and guides the activity and is the equating force.

Sharing time can be a vital source of learning through

communication. Unfortunately it often degenerates into something less than that. If the teacher attempts to use sharing time for a desk-cleaning or lesson-planning period, the children are likely to wander aimlessly from braggadocio to boredom. Unless the teacher supplies motive and power, sharing time will be nothing more than a mildly pleasant interlude before books are opened and mouths are closed.

## CREATIVE DRAMATICS

As a general term, *creative dramatics* has been defined as an activity which "includes all types of informal drama improvised by the players."[1] In its application to the elementary school, creative dramatics provides an opportunity for free verbalization on the child's level of ability. Much of what is termed creative dramatics is improvised and initiated within the classroom and remains there. At times the teacher employs creative dramatics as a method for devising an assembly program. When an assembly program is anticipated, the original dialogue of the children is written down, costumes and scenery are designed by the children, and "creative dramatics" becomes a more or less formal "play." It loses much of its spontaneity and originality in this transition and becomes much more stylized. The emphasis regarding oral communication shifts from extemporization to rigid recital. For this reason teachers try to keep creative dramatics within the framework of classroom participation only.

A unit on almost any subject can be used as the basis for creating a story. A dramatic play of colonial America based

[1] Winifred Ward, "Creative Dramatics," in *The Role of Speech in the Elementary School*, edited by the Speech Association of America. Washington: National Education Association, 1951, p. 76.

on the group's study of early American history is often improvised. Even kindergartners, with the fine imagination of
the untrammeled five-year-old mind, can devise a multitude
of dramatic incidents revolving around, for example, a trip
to the farm. Another area for creative dramatics can center
around social situations and pressures encountered by the
child at his particular age or school level. Real-life situations
can be dramatized. Reënactments of problems which con-
front the children in their everyday life will give actors as
well as observers a new and more objective attitude. Although rarely used for such a purpose, creative dramatics
might be an excellent mode of speech hygiene. Children
need help in learning how to react to the big boy who bullies
the playground; the child who teases and runs away; the
one who snatches away another's personal belongings. "Play
acting" out of such problems and their solutions can be an
aid to the child's emotional development as well as a release device.

Puppets and marionettes are also used as a form of creative
dramatics. These props are especially valuable to children
who find it difficult to speak before a group in person. Children who become self-conscious and speechless when required
to appear or perform in front of a group need the protection
afforded by the stage and the puppets. With this camou-
flage they can then use the opportunity for "play acting." A
great deal of release and play therapy is performed clinically
through the use of dolls and puppets and an adaptation of
this therapy can be carried on in the classroom through the
same medium. Puppets resembling favorite television performers can be used by the children to express the pent-up

hostilities and emotions of their manipulators without social stigma.

## GROUP PLANNING AND REPORTS

New trends in education have swept away some of the cobwebs of autocratic control in the classroom. Coöperative planning between pupils and teacher is gaining favor. Teachers who have tried it have found that children gain something more than academic knowledge when they are allowed to plan and work on projects in small groups. This is not to imply that the teacher relinquishes her control of the classroom; far from it. She now attempts a much more difficult form of control. Hers must be a more subtle approach, wherein she directs and guides and maintains discipline as a democratic leader rather than an autocratic ruler.

At one time such a democratic approach was thought feasible only for "student councils" and other student governing bodies with little or no real authority. However, such councils have shown that they can function as an integrated group and with a minimum of assistance from the teacher. In some schools, student courts are formed even at the elementary level and pupils are brought before them when infractions of school rules occur. Approval or penalization by one's classmates has a powerful effect on pupil behavior. The teacher often finds that peer discipline is not only more effective but more easily tolerated by her children. Pupil participation in planning and executing projects has been extended from merely social and extracurricular activities to include many academic objectives as well.

No longer need American history be assigned by the

teacher in this manner: "Read Chapters Ten and Eleven in your text and answer the questions at the end of the chapters for tomorrow." The modern teacher and her children will plan to use the material in those chapters as a basis for a coöperative project, such as construction of a miniature covered wagon scene, an exhibit of Indian costumes, a play about the westward movement, a debate concerning the rights of the red man, or a charitable campaign to help the Navahos on their reservations.

In conducting such a project, a pupil chairman may be chosen by the class. He in turn appoints committees to carry out the various activities, most of which will involve group participation. A committee may be appointed to construct a covered wagon train and paint the scenery for a display on the library table; a committee to read and report on other books about Indians; a costume committee to make appropriate crepe-paper apparel if a play or story is to be dramatized; and perhaps a committee to compose an original play or story of pioneering America. Throughout the whole unit runs the opportunity to increase the oral communicative skills of the youngsters, but the teacher often feels that because of curricular pressures she must concentrate on getting across the academic material. Many times she has chosen the method of pupil participation and planning because she has observed how well it has worked out in another classroom, how effective it is in stirring up and maintaining the interest of the children and in motivating them to read and to learn more. Much of the learning under this type of classroom procedure will come through student reports, student recitations, student discussion, and student plays, all of which implies a great need for adequate oral communication. Yet the stress is usually placed on the material rather than its presentation, and this is as it should be.

However, we are all aware of individuals who are unable to present their thinking effectively, to hold the interest of a group, merely because their speech habits are poor. If this is true on the adult level, it is doubly true with children who are in the process of acquiring academic knowledge as well as more mature speech patterns. When the reporting student is inadequate in his speech skills, the rest of the class learns little. Although the teacher may state that the primary goal is transfer of information, this goal cannot be accomplished without a great deal of attention to the communicative values inherent in this kind of teaching. We must help our children to communicate effectively if we want to teach in this manner.

### GROUP PROBLEM SOLVING

When the whole class or a segment of the class attempts to solve a specific problem, the primary goal for both teacher and pupils would appear to be the satisfactory solution of the problem. The interpersonal relationships involved in such a group attack on a problem and the social adjustments which must be made by the various members of the class are often cited as reason enough for such a methodology.

"What can we do to stop snowballing on the playground?" might be considered a realistic problem for a group of first- or second-graders. The group, after discussing the problem orally, may formulate a set of rules for their class which will be written or posted on the bulletin board. While the actual formulation of the rules may be the crystallization of all previous discussion, most of the actual social learning occurred during the period when the children did their talking. They became interested as they talked. If snowballing should not be allowed on the playground, where would it be safe? How can they help others who might forget the rules? The degree to which this or any other problem is solved depends largely on the degree to which the children are able to understand and evaluate each other's ideas through oral communication. We certainly provide the need for oral communication in our modern schools, but we do little to improve it enough to make it truly effective.

## AUDIO-VISUAL AIDS

While motion pictures have been used for years by the school as entertainment during assembly programs and other school functions, it has been only recently that the movies have left the auditorium for the classroom. Slides, film strips, and 16 mm. films cover an overwhelming variety of subjects. We need such audio-visual aids to learning. Some schools have been installing television sets, and as the channels reserved for educational stations come into use, more undoubtedly will be found in the classroom. All of these, besides the other communicative media such as the radio and newspaper, are used as teaching as well as motivating devices.

The use of almost any of the above-mentioned aids has been routinized by the teacher to follow this kind of cycle: (1) Discuss it; (2) use it; (3) rediscuss it. It is felt that the children will learn more if they are "briefed" first, usually by the teacher, on what they are going to listen to or watch. Then the television program, slides, film strip, or motion pictures are shown, followed by a class discussion. During this period the teacher attempts to get the children to contribute and to verbalize. A picture is said to be worth a thousand explanatory words. The discussions that precede and follow provide several times that amount.

If possible, the teacher attempts to have the content of films or other audio-visual material closely allied to a project or unit under way in the classroom. This can be accomplished even at the kindergarten or first-grade level. For example, if a unit on boats is being presented, the children bring pictures of boats, the teacher reads stories about boats, they sing songs about boats, listen to records about boats, see movies and film strips about boats, and finally, if the exhausted teacher's stamina is sufficient, even build a boat from building blocks and use it for a "creative dramatics" shipwreck scene. Everything from kayaks to the S.S. *America* becomes material for learning. The oral communicative values of such a procedure can well be imagined, but unfortunately, the child is often regarded as a sponge which must be made to soak up as much factual information as possible, to be squeezed out drop by drop at the appropriate moment.

Recordings are now being used by the classroom teacher to present good music, to stimulate interest in musical instruments, to supplement the songs she is attempting to teach, and to teach rhythms. Interpreting music through bodily activity is a favorite diversion of young children. They march, prance, strut, sway, and gallop, but seldom do they vocalize while doing rhythms in the classroom. Here, too, is an opportunity for the use of speech sounds.

The teacher lucky enough to have access to a tape recorder has a limitless expanse of auditory impressions at her command. She can use it in all types of oral communication projects to identify, to illustrate, to define. The tape recorder is most valuable perhaps when it is used to record classroom events, planned or unplanned. The spontaneity and individuality thus recorded is a guarantee of high listener ratings.

## LISTENING

So much of what we know and learn is brought to us through our ears that it is a wonder that somewhere during our educational journey we do not have a course entitled "Beginning Listening." Teachers of deaf and hard-of-hearing youngsters are aware of the "listening" problem even more than normal classroom teachers are. Teachers of acoustically handicapped children must find a substitute way of communicating with their children. For the 80 percent of learning that the hearing child gains through the use of his ears the deaf child must substitute visual "hearing."

Our conversations are liberally sprinkled with "I said . . ." and "he said . . . ," or, much more modestly, with "I read. . . ." That we often listen inaccurately, even when we are attempting to be attentive, is distressingly obvious. An excellent example is the game wherein a whispered message travels down a row of people to emerge at the end of the row in such garbled form that the originator might do well to disown it. If this be true of adults, with their longer auditory memory span, greater concentration powers, and wider experience, think of the children in the classroom. They are not equipped with adult minds—or ears—and yet they are usually expected to absorb much of what is said to them. To listen with understanding and discrimination is difficult. Teachers who are aware of their children's present listening limitations will try to help them increase their abilities to understand, to discriminate, to "listen."

## GETTING THE CHILD TO TALK AND LISTEN

How do we teachers usually go about helping children grow in their ability to communicate with others? Good teachers are already using devices like those just discussed in their attempts to provide a wide variety of communicative experiences. They are constantly searching for new methods. They know that increased ability in oral communication is an important asset, and one which pays high dividends in and out of the classroom. Adequacy in oral communication facilitates transfer of information for it represents a basis of understanding. Children in the early elementary grades often communicate on a somewhat crude and inefficient level. They find it difficult to express themselves and to explain their thoughts and feelings to others. They may be able to comprehend but they cannot command the language of the adult. This low level of intercommunication, by adult standards at least, results in an inadequate and incomplete transfer of information. Since teaching and talking are often synonymous, every child needs to increase his ability to communicate orally.

Creative dramatics, sharing time, group problem solving, audio-visual devices, and the other types of activities which have been discussed do *provide an opportunity* to help children learn to communicate more successfully. However, the opportunity thus provided is usually exploited by those students who, comparatively speaking, already have greater ability, while children who need to improve their skills too often remain silent. On occasion the teacher may note this silence and make spasmodic attempts to help the child who is deficient in speech skills. This help is often extended on an emergency basis only, with little or no planning preceding or following the incident. We need a planned program to teach the orally clumsy child to keep from falling over his verbal feet. It should not be limited, however, to such children, for every child in the room deserves and benefits from a comprehensive speech improvement program. Let us then provide more than the *opportunity* to increase communication skills; let us provide *actual speech experiences* for each child in the classroom.

Each of the activities that have been mentioned, as well as many new and different ones, can serve as learning experiences to master the communicative skills. Let us look again at the various activities now being used. This time we will consider each in the light of a good speech improvement program. Each activity will stress improvement of oral communication skills as its primary goal, with transfer of information as a no less vital, but secondary, objective. Good speech and good learning can be blood brothers.

## AN IMPROVED SHARING TIME

How can the teacher handle the sharing or telling time period so that it will provide the greatest benefit as an oral communication activity? Sharing time is ideally suited for this purpose since it can be twin-pronged in its approach. It may serve as a speech improvement period and a "training in listening" period as well.

Sharing time is, in essence, a voluntary speech situation. More than that, it is an unrehearsed speech experience, in that the child who chooses to speak during sharing time has no "set" speech, even at times no clear-cut idea that he wants to present. This very vagueness can be a blessing in disguise. This is the child's chance to learn something about speaking on his feet, organizing his thoughts rapidly, and presenting a coherent picture of his ideas. Needless to say, he does not learn all this through one or two experiences during sharing time, nor can he do it alone. The teacher's guidance, not dictation, is required.

The elementary teacher often finds that she has a few children who consistently and repeatedly volunteer for sharing time, and the rest of the class remains in the role of unhappy draftees. These children lack the necessary self-confidence to stand before the rest of the class and speak coherently. How does the teacher help a draftee to volunteer?

First of all, she realizes that she must often help these children on a nonverbal level before she can hope to have them improve their verbal performance. Then, too, she must recognize the source of a child's refusal to participate in this kind of speech activity. If she knows why the child refuses or is reluctant to join in, she can better determine by what means she can aid him. Verbalizing for the child is an excellent method for helping such a child at first. Here is one teacher's suggestion for helping a little girl in her room:

If Mary comes to you at the beginning of the day and shyly hands you a doll in Norwegian dress and whispers that her uncle brought it to her, you might first suggest that you will be glad to help her when sharing time begins. If Mary demurs, you can point out to her that she will have the important job of holding the doll so that all the boys and girls can see it, and pointing out the special kind of costume the doll is wearing. Encourage Mary to tell you as much as she will about how she felt when her uncle gave her the doll and about the country the doll came from. Then, when Mary is holding the doll in her arms and is standing beside you during sharing time, talk for her to the rest of the class. Do this, not as the teacher, but rather as Mary. You will use the words that she would use could she but find the courage. This is not the time to teach about Norway. Do that another time. *This* is the time to help Mary become confident enough to enter a speech situation. You do this by being Mary's interpreter; by watching her as you speak; by using the cues she provides by her facial expression and body position. And most of all, there is to be no censoring expression or feeling on your part that Mary is inadequate because she cannot perform as you would like to have her perform. Perhaps all that Mary needs is this one lift over the speech barrier. She may break into your monologue with comments of her own. As a matter of fact, you want to provide opportunity for this spontaneous speech to occur and to make her feel that this is a joint venture. . . . "Mary has brought something to show you today. While Mary holds the doll up and turns it around so that all of you may see it, we'll tell you something about it. Mary's uncle just came back from a far-away country. It's called Norway. Your uncle had to cross the ocean to come home, didn't he, Mary? He came across on a big . . . let's see, Mary, oh, yes, he took a boat home. He brought this beautiful doll with him. You've given your doll a name . . . it's . . . oh, yes, Marta." Mary may not use this opportunity to talk, but you've paved the way for future speech attempts.

Mary's teacher was trying to devise a bridge over which the child could cross from silence to communication. Verbalizing for the child is just one method for accomplishing this goal. "Self-talk" can also be used as a bridge. Talking to oneself, in this case, is not indicative of an unbalanced state of mind but rather is a method used daily by children and occasionally by adults to accompany and emphasize their thoughts. And more adults would use self-talk more frequently if they were not afraid of being overheard.

The teacher can demonstrate "self-talk" to her group as a whole in a manner similar to this:

You know, when I make up a story in my head, I often say the words out loud because I like the way they feel as I say them. And I often talk out loud even when I'm not making up a story. . . . I talk when I cook, like saying, "Oh, I forgot to salt the stew" even when there's no one in the kitchen to hear me. We all think in words so it's really no different to say the words we think out loud. I'm going to plant some seeds now and show you what I mean: "I pick up an empty coffee can. . . . I put it next to the soil on the newspaper. . . . I put the soil in the can and now I sprinkle these seeds on top of the soil. . . . I'll put one here and one here and some here. Now I put a little more dirt on top of the seeds. I take the watering can and pour some water over all the dirt." Bob, here is another can and some flower seeds; let's try and see if you can do self-talk, too.

There are usually some children in each classroom who exist in a no man's land or "fringe area" of group activity. They are the children who have few friendships with others in the group. They are the isolates of the sociogram. With these children, the teacher's first goal is to help them become part of the group. They often need to be nonverbal members of the group before they can become verbal participants.

The teacher is often able to give the child status by having him perform activities which are prized by his peers. Stacking the chairs, leading the group down the hall, watering the plants, carrying the milk cartons, being in charge of eraser-cleaning—all these and many more nonverbal activities can represent belonging as well as leadership. Once the child's place in the group is secure, he is ready to cross the speech bridge and explore further areas of oral communication.

For example, Jimmy is a second-grader who shows little or no interest in sharing time. He wiggles and squirms and pokes his neighbors. His teacher has been trying to find ways of interesting him but with little success. Today, however, she asked him to help her put up some new pictures on the bulletin board. At the end of sharing time, she said, "Jimmy and I worked hard this morning before most of you came to school and we put some pictures on the board that I know you'll be interested in. They're pictures of Deer Forest, the place we are going to visit next week. Jimmy, please go over to the bulletin board and point to the picture of the place *you* would like to see first when we reach Deer Forest. Oh, you want to see where the deer eat and drink? Now, the rest of you may choose, one at a time, the place you'd like to see first and Jimmy will help by pointing to the picture so we all know exactly what we will be looking for. Oh, Jimmy, would you make a mark on the paper underneath each picture when someone chooses it? That way we'll know the places that interest us the most." After everyone had chosen his favorite place to visit, the teacher asked, "Jimmy, would you count the number of marks underneath each picture and tell us how many want to visit each place?"

During the next few weeks the teacher asked Jimmy to participate in some group speech performances, such as taking part in a pantomime while another child read a story, reading in unison with the rest of the reading group, or singing a jingle with two or three other children. Jimmy gained confidence slowly but steadily through a myriad of group speech activities.

Finally, the teacher used sharing time as Jimmy's first real attempt at an individual speech activity. She asked Jimmy to show the rest of the class the cloth picture he had made the previous day during art period. Jimmy stood before the class. Silence descended. An encouraging nod from the teacher and Jimmy hesitatingly began, "I . . . I made this picture yesterday. I . . . ah . . . uh . . . it's made outa cloth. Uh . . . it's pasted on paper." Great oratory? Perhaps not, but Jimmy has taken his first step toward more adequate oral communication. The next time he stands before the class, it may be to give a more detailed report on how he uses his mono-view space mask in playing space cadets. With each speech activity he becomes more proficient if he is able to build on a solid foundation of confidence and ease.

For those children who feel no reticence about standing before the group and talking, sharing time can be a valuable experience in learning how to talk in the most effective manner—or perhaps how to listen. This does not mean that the teacher must stop and correct the child after every mispronounced or misarticulated word. Rather, the teacher should again determine the areas in which the child needs the most help and then use the sharing time period to foster growth in this area. Since Susan's voice is no more than a whisper when she stands before the class, her turn at sharing time was preceded with: "Susan, when you talk to us today, look at Ann who is sitting in the back of the room. Pretend to be talking straight to Ann and be sure that she hears you. Ann, would you raise your hand when you can't hear what Susan is saying? Thank you. Now, Susan, tell us about your new puppy and let's see if we can make Ann keep her hand down for the whole time." Susan spoke clearly and loudly at first, but her voice soon dwindled to its accustomed intensity. Ann's hand shot up, but Susan didn't see it. The teacher quietly moved to the back of the room and stood behind Ann. Susan, aware of the motion, again raised her voice. When she finished her story of the puppy's first night in her home, the teacher helped her to evaluate her speech. "It was pretty hard to talk loudly enough all the time, wasn't it, Susan? It looks as though we'll need more practice, but you certainly did well this time. Ann only got the chance to raise her hand twice!"

Another method for giving the talkative youngsters a variety of speech activities is to carry out a program of intergroup telling. The class is split up into smaller segments, each led by a child who has the ability to play the teacher role. These groups participate in miniature sharing time periods. Even in the small groups, the teacher role is then rotated so that every child eventually has the opportunity to participate in intergroup telling.

### AN IMPROVED CREATIVE DRAMATICS PROGRAM

The primary purpose of creative dramatics is self-expression rather than formalized drama, as was discussed earlier in this chapter. The teacher who uses creative dramatics to teach communication skills must employ an indirect approach. The spontaneity that makes this activity so engaging will not be lost or its learning possibilities hindered if the teacher restricts her guidance to one or two essential points.

An inherent value of creative dramatics which is rarely exploited is its great possibilities for mental hygiene through speech. Children can create and act out stories that have some emotional significance for them. That this emotional significance may often be cloaked in fantasy does not reduce its value for either children or teacher. The children receive a great deal of release through expressing their true feelings even in a disguised form, and the teacher who is perceptive will still gain insight into the children's problems and needs. Many of the favorite fairy tales and fables are based on the kind of problems that children have today. All sorts of misadventures occur in these stories because children wander away from home or tell untruths or do forbidden things. Children unconsciously compare their mother's saying, "Do not speak to strangers on the street!" with Little Red Riding Hood's chat with the wolf, Alice's conversation with the Wonderland rabbit, or Hansel and Gretel's nearly fatal fascination with the Gingerbread House in the woods. The teacher certainly need not insist that the children use such stories intact, but they may serve as the basis for a session of creative dramatics. In fact, just where and how the children alter such a story, the emotions they disclose while portraying the characters in the story, and their use of speech and expression may be very revealing.

If the children think of their classroom as a fairly permissive place, this garb of fantasy need not always be employed. The children might act out the story of a little boy whose Mommy and Daddy made him sleep in a dark room even though he was terribly afraid of all the animal shadows who lived there when the light in the hall was turned off. Or the story of a little girl who took some money from her mother's purse to buy some candy and then was afraid to tell anyone about it. This kind of creative dramatics cannot stem wholly and directly from the teacher, however. The children must feel free and willing to act out such true-to-life problems and be able to express their thoughts without fear of censorship by the teacher. The fact that the children are acting in a "play" should make it possible for her to remove herself from the role of judge and jury.

Should only the children with the most vivid imaginations and nimblest tongues be used as actors in creative dramatics? We hope not, especially if creative dramatics is to serve a mental hygiene purpose. Most teachers are well aware of the more blatant "behavior problems" in their room. However, there are those children who are so quiet and so conforming as to fade almost out of the teacher's sight—and mind. Many teachers now use the sociogram to give them a more accurate picture of their classroom social structure and its constantly changing focus. The sociogram is a schematic diagram showing how many times one child chooses another within a given period or for a particular event. A teacher may use such a simple question as "Whom do you want to sit next to you during the party this afternoon?" Each child may write his answer or perhaps tell the teacher privately. Some children are consistently chosen many times, while others have a few friends, and one or two may not be chosen at all. The latter are rejected by the other members of the classroom and their isolated position is clearly demonstrated in such a schematic design. A series of speech sociograms taken throughout the school year will demonstrate whether or not these isolated children are being accepted more readily by the other members of the class. Certainly the sociogram results should be used by the teacher in planning group activities. Selecting a cast of players for creative dramatics is one method of utilizing those children who need the opportunity thus provided for "belonging" to the group. The children who exist on the fringe of the social group also need the creative dramatics activity as a means of release from the tension which is generated by being an outsider.

Teaching communication skills through creative dramatics can also be accomplished in a much more direct fashion. The teacher may offer direct guidance, for example, in suggesting to a youngster who portrays a fairy that such miniature creatures would undoubtedly have small, high voices. Another child might be shown that, in his role of a Christmas church bell, a large bell makes a deep and sonorous *ding dong* rather than the squeaky *din don* of his present performance. Such explanations or discussions are not interjected into the play itself. The use of pitch, inflection, and speech rhythm to reflect feeling is discussed only after the play period is over, and much of this can still be done indirectly. The teacher could comment: "Did you notice how John helped us to understand about the boy he was pretending to be? He showed us by his voice that the boy in the play was mad at his mother for refusing to let him go with the other boys. You know, when you feel mad inside, your voice trembles and becomes very loud and angry sounding. So when we are pretending to be mad, we don't talk in a little voice, we shout!—just the way the boy in the play shouted at his mother."

## BETTER GROUP PLANNING AND REPORTS

When the classroom teacher uses the group planning approach for teaching academic material, she finds that most of the learning takes place through speech—hers and her students'. Group planning involves, and evolves out of, group *discussion*. It also spotlights speech skills. Each child must be able to use his speech to command the attention of the group.

This can be a highly competitive speech situation. Training in competitive communication is certainly invaluable in our verbal environment. Most children must compete for their parents' attention through our modern sound barrier: a radio or television program, a baby's caterwaul, a telephone's ring, or the chatter of the next-door neighbor who dropped in for a cup of coffee.

Group or panel discussions can teach the art of graceful interruption as well as the polite denial of such interruption. Speech competition, wisely guided by the teacher, can help each child improve his communication skills. The teacher might purposely let chaos reign during a group discussion for a short period of time. Upon restoring order she can suggest that the chairman of the discussion group, with the help of the other children, write on the blackboard the reasons why the talking got out of hand and list some better ways of handling such a situation. The group may not come up with a complete *Robert's Rules of Order*, but they will devise a system to keep speech competition under control. And, equally important, the children will devise methods for resisting interruption.

Recitation and reports offer a highly specific method for improving children's speech. The teacher can set up a precise goal. For example, a fourth-grade boy who is working on a slight lingual lisp is going to read a report on the local Soap Box Derby. The teacher's suggestion is: "Jim, when you read us your report this afternoon, I'd like to hear you say *ssssoap* instead of *tho*ap each time you mention the derby. I know that you can use a good *ssss* sound if you are careful. Let's underline the word *soap* in your report and every time you come to it, prolong the sss sound slightly. I'll keep score for you on a little pad of paper as you go along and we'll check it together after you've finished."

## BETTER GROUP PROBLEM SOLVING

In group problem solving each student theoretically contributes to the best of his ability. We would like to point out that he need not contribute in the academic area in which he is superior. Would it not be wise to use the group problem approach as an incentive to learn rather than a reward for knowledge already acquired?

For example, if the best readers in the room do all the reading on the problem while the best students in mathematics do all the calculations involved and the best speakers give all the conclusions, group problem solving will have little to offer the majority of class members other than a spectator role. Their imagination and interest will not be stirred if it is a foregone conclusion that the "brains" in the room will get all the credit. If we are to use group problem solving for speech improvement purposes, we cannot limit oral work to those children with a flair for fluency. How much it would mean to a stutterer to be able to participate without penalty in a panel discussion on the building of model airplanes, even though he might not be the most expert airplane hobbyist in the room!

The group approach is an excellent nucleus speech situation, since the amount of speech and the degree of success can be more accurately predicted under these circumstances. If the problem be mathematical, the girl with a lisp can use this situation to practice a good *s* sound when she shows how to multiply "six (siks) times seven." In this way she learns to use correct articulation in normal everyday speech situations. It is a highly conscious and motivated sort of speech performance and will have a great deal more effect than hours of drill, saying such words as "silk, six, sock, seven, soup, stop" over and over again to herself or to the teacher. With a little forethought, the teacher can use a group problem-solving situation for helping several children improve their speech skills. She is in a position to help each child make some self-assignment to be carried out during the situation, and she is also in a position to help the child judge the results of such assignments. And the teacher and child directly concerned need not do this assignment and the subsequent judging in a secretive manner. An atmosphere of careful and critical, though never censorious, listening can be developed on the part of all the children in the room.

Since every child will benefit from a planned program of speech improvement, every child in the class should have an opportunity to participate in self-assignments and self-judgments. Each child should be encouraged to design a speech assignment which will be helpful to him, under the guidance of the teacher.

Judging the success of such a speech assignment can be an individual or a group affair. If the child is secure in his relationships with the other children in the room, group evaluation of his speech assignment is not only possible but profitable. However, the teacher may feel that some children, at least in the beginning, would profit more from a more private evaluation. The child may be asked to evaluate alone his own progress, or the evaluation might be jointly accomplished by child and teacher, or two or three other children could be called upon to help judge, along with the child, his speech assignment.

Student-conducted meetings are often quite demonstrative

as well as being democratic. They provide a natural method for helping the children who participate to speak and think on their feet. Competition, in these meetings, is at the peer level, and the children are not subject to an adult's speech competence. This may result in a "no holds barred" attitude on the part of the student, but if the teacher can control herself and remain in the background, the children will learn a great deal about intelligent and impromptu speaking. Group approval is a strong motivating force among elementary-age children, and in this type of speech situation adequate or superior speaking will be thus rewarded. When increased ability to communicate is rewarded by the admiration of fellow classmates, there is a strong stimulus toward even greater speech competence.

## ADDITIONAL USES OF AUDIO-VISUAL AIDS

As was shown previously, the technique for presenting audio-visual material has been standarized into a talk-see-talk or talk-listen-talk routine. During the time film strip, record, movie, or slides are being shown or listened to, children are expected to remain silent. Especially with the film strips or slides which are often used in the lower elementary grades, the teacher provides the running commentary, if any. Any remark by a child is likely to be squashed with a sharp "shhhhh." If the child is talking without saying anything, that is one thing. But if the child has an urgent desire to communicate some bit of information or knowledge which is pertinent, that is a distinctly different matter. Would it not be wise to let him make his contribution when it has its highest interest value? His desire to communicate is at a peak at that moment and may wane completely by the time all the films or all the slides have been shown and the teacher has summarized what she has found important. How many adults know the experience of being in the midst of a group conversation, with something they would like to contribute, and yet feel themselves frustrated because the appropriate moment for the comment comes and goes? What was important ten minutes ago loses all its savor when the conversation takes a different tack or someone else decisively closes the issue. Let us use the interest generated by audio-visual techniques to stimulate improved speech.

The teacher can select children from the group in advance or on the spot to give word pictures of what they are viewing or listening to. Perhaps a child can be "briefed" to present a few slides and supply the verbal side dish. Many teachers have found that children can prepare slides of their own which, while crude, are extremely effective.

The teacher usually has plenty of opportunities to talk in an audience situation, while the children have very few. Audio-visual material can be used to help the latter gain experience and to improve their communication skills through actual practice.

### SUMMARY

Children need more than the *opportunity* to develop speech skills. They need to *experiment* with actual speech experiences. It is up to the teacher to provide and to integrate these experiences into her daily program. It is her job to help the children make the fullest possible use of these experiences. The teacher's most effective teaching often comes through talking. Much of her children's learning comes through increased skill in oral communication.

# III
## *Speech Improvement Time*

🌂   "SPEECH improvement? How can I teach speech improvement? And when? Why, sometimes I can't get all my reading groups in!" In the busy schedule of the elementary teacher there never seems to be enough time to do half the things she wishes to accomplish. Then, too, the teacher may feel that the children are inclined to spend enough time "talking," with or without her permission. To propose that she set aside fifteen or twenty minutes of her day for speech improvement may at first seem to be merely crowding the hours with another activity, laudable enough in itself but hardly of such vital importance as to require its insertion into the curriculum.

However, in experimenting with these programs, we have found no classroom teacher who ever discontinued a speech improvement program once she had participated in one. The period spent in improving oral communication eased the teacher's burdens rather than increased them. Here are some of the comments:

I must admit I was very reluctant to start the speech improvement class. I didn't know too much about speech, really. I felt that the unison activities might get out of hand and that they would have the children too excited. But once we started, it became my favorite time of the whole day. The children were always calmer afterwards and seemed to work better. I was able to reach children this way that were hard to get to in any other way. And what is more, they certainly loved it.

I found the reading improved and I think because of the speech improvement period. Children became interested in words and the vocal phonics activities certainly fascinated them. You could see the change in their spelling attitudes, too.

What I found most striking was the immediate increase in volunteering. Boys and girls who before seldom talked in class now were taking part. And they expressed themselves better. I know our class discussions became much freer and more pupils took part in them. Another thing, after we'd been doing the speech improvement for a while, more children came to me with their troubles or school problems.

I still don't see why the children enjoy the speech improvement period so much. It certainly must satisfy some deep need that they have but I don't know what it is. Perhaps it's because they all feel equal and free from competition, or maybe it's because the activities shift so quickly from one surprising thing to another. They look forward to the unexpected. I know they certainly wait for speech improvement time and wish it came oftener than twice a week.

## WHY TEACH COMMUNICATION SKILLS?

In the previous chapter we described many of the ways by which classroom teachers attempt to improve the oral communication skills of their pupils. As described in the first part of the chapter, the large majority of these are indirect methods and are often relatively inefficient. They provide opportunity for speech improvement but no goals. What increase in communicative skills does occur is more a by-product than a direct result. This would not be so unfortunate in itself if these speaking opportunities were not also productive of such bad habits as halting fluency, inadequate expression of thought, incoherent expression of feelings, weak or unpleasant voices, and sloppy enunciation. In our society the ability to express oneself verbally with ease and vividness brings many returns. Individuals who have little communicative skill do not get these rewards, and it is a reflection upon our schools that we teach these skills so poorly. More drastic measures are necessary. We no longer dare hope that merely providing plenty of opportunity for talking or discussion will solve this problem. In the latter part of the previous chapter we mentioned a few ways in which these self-same activities could be used for speech improvement. It has become apparent that these, plus many more activities, must be used to fulfill our obligation to help children improve their communication skills. To accomplish such a goal we must devote at least a small portion of our limited school time toward the attainment of communicative proficiency.

## CORRELATING SPEECH WITH OTHER ACTIVITIES

As the teacher reviews her daily schedule, she will note several periods during which speech improvement may be logically integrated into her program. Phonic workbooks as an adjunct to reading are often ideal sources from which an oral, as well as written, sound lesson can be constructed. A music period may stress vocalized rhythm and variations in pitch and volume. A spelling lesson enables the teacher to introduce new words not only for accurate written reproduction but also for accurate articulation. Units in English or social studies may deal with the use of the telephone or introducing people. Such units lend themselves with ease to speech improvement. Even an art class can be used for speech improvement since children often tell the "story behind the picture."

## SPEECH IMPROVEMENT IN RELATION TO SPEECH THERAPY

While correlation with other subject areas is profitable and often possible, a separate speech improvement period in which the whole class participates can have even greater value and can help the speech correction program which may exist in the school. It serves as an excellent basis for individual and group speech therapy at a later date. The normal-speaking children in the room are more easily motivated to help, not hinder, the speech-defective child. "Going to speech class" becomes an extension of an activity which all in the classroom have participated in and have enjoyed. The speech defective's classmates no longer regard him as one who is "a baby" or "too dumb" to speak correctly. The whole group is oriented more favorably toward speech therapy. Even if there is no speech correctionist in the system, speech improvement periods in the classroom will aid the classroom teacher in establishing right attitudes in her children. The children are able to understand that faulty speech need no longer be a disgrace. Because of their peer relationship, they are capable of serving as helpers or teachers. Even kindergartners can remind a classmate that he's "pointed his tongue" when saying an *s* word. A first-grader can understand that just as Johnny has difficulty in counting to twenty and Mary writes a *b* and *d* backwards, just so does Susie find it difficult to distinguish between "wabbit" and "rabbit" or "sicken" and "chicken."

A speech improvement period in which the entire class participates will result in greater understanding and more adequate speech on the part of all.

### THE SPEECH IMPROVEMENT PERIOD

In instituting a speech improvement program, the first questions which must be faced are these: "How much time will be required for an efficient speech improvement period?" and "In what grades should it be instituted?"

We have experimented with periods of different durations and frequency and we find that excellent results can be achieved in from twenty to thirty minutes on a once- or twice-a-week basis. In some schools speech improvement periods are held daily, while in others only one period per week is devoted exclusively to training in oral communication. We feel that some time should be devoted directly to speech improvement in all of the elementary grades, but that the greatest returns come from such training in the kindergarten and grades one through four. The effectiveness of any program, of course, depends largely upon the enthusiasm and ability of the teacher. In some schools the speech improvement period replaces the sharing time or the oral English period once or twice each week. In others it is given a definite place in the curriculum. In all schools the value of such a program is recognized.

Specialists in the development of speech have discovered that the average child's speech is not mature when he enters kindergarten, and that a great many articulation errors remain throughout first and perhaps second grade. It is this very immaturity of speech which poses many problems for the teachers of early elementary classes. The kindergarten teacher especially is usually concerned with the speech of the children in her group. She often finds one or two children whose speech is very difficult to understand and many others who exhibit varying degrees of articulation errors. Kindergarten teachers often find that a short speech improvement period three or four times a week helps immensely with the reading readiness program.

## AN EXAMPLE OF A TYPICAL SPEECH IMPROVEMENT PERIOD

In order to give a picture of the speech improvement program in action, we quote the following observer's report from stenographic transcription. This particular session was held in a first-grade room shortly after the beginning of the second semester. It was conducted by the regular classroom teacher.

1:10.  *Teacher:* Everyone stand up and play Follow the Speech Leader game. Watch me and say what I say and do what I do. Ready! (She wets her finger and holds it horizontally along her lower lip.) Cool my finger with a *fffffff*. Cool my finger with a *fffffff*. (She bites her teeth and smiles and shakes her head.) I bite and smile and say *sssss*. I bite and smile and say *sssss*. (She places her fingers on her throat, opens her mouth wide.) I tuck my tongue down and say *kuh-kuh-kuh*. I tuck my tongue down and say *kuh-kuh-kuh*.

1:13.  *Teacher:* Everybody sit down. Here's a guessing game. Point to the thing I'm saying. Point to your *sh* - - - - -

*oe.* Point to your *nnnn – – – – – oh – – – – – zzzzz.* Point
to my *fffff – – – – – eeeee – – – – t.* Good!

1:15. *Teacher:* See this little man? He doesn't talk quite right.
He wants you to help him say his words better. (She
uses a fist puppet and assumes a falsetto voice, pausing
slightly after each mispronounced word.) *Puppet:* I like
ice kween . . . cones. I like tochalate . . . ice cream
best. My mother says I eat too mutts. . . . (Children
correct puppet.) Thank you for helping me today.
Good-by!

1:17. *Teacher:* Everybody put your elbows on your desk like
this. Now hold your chin in both hands, like this. Now
let's try to wiggle our tongues up and down as we say
*la – la – la* without moving our chins or heads. Just move
the tongue alone. Here we go . . . let's do it once
more.

1:19. *Teacher:* Now let's see if we can't have some fun. Let's
see how long you can keep talking. Let's talk slowly but
keep it going. Tell me just what I am doing. I'll show
you: "Teacher sits down. Teacher gets a pencil and puts
it in her hair. She takes it out and writes on a piece of
paper. She puts the pencil down. She tears the paper up
and puts it in the basket." Remember not to hurry.
Ready? (Teacher went through the same routine, adding
several new activities to those previously demonstrated.)

1:22. *Teacher:* You know, some people's voices are nice and
others just don't sound so good. I'm going to use some
poor voices and one good voice. Whenever I use a poor
voice, I want you to shake your head. When I use my
nice voice, clap your hands. (She demonstrates several
poor voices: strident, nasal, hoarse, and then a pleasant
one. The children respond appropriately.) *Teacher:* Now
say, "I don't like you!" in your poor voice.

1:26. *Teacher:* I wonder if you can talk like a giant? Giants talk way down here (she lowers her pitch) but they also talk very loud. Let's be a giant and say: "I am a giant. Ho! Hoh! HOH!" Let's do it again.

1:30. *Teacher:* I want to tell you a story. Once upon a time there was a little first-grader who used to get so tired in school that he didn't know what to do. He tried hard to sit still but he . . . _____ yes, he wiggled and moved around and looked out of the _____ yes, window. He even forgot sometimes that he was in _____ yes, school. One day his teacher was tired too and when she called his _____, yes, name, and he didn't answer, she told him he must learn to pay _____ yes, attention. But he just couldn't. All he wanted to do was to go out to _____ yes, play, or go home to see his _____ that's right, mother. But then one day he began to like school and everything turned out all right. I wonder if you can guess what happened? When we play this game next week, I'll tell you.

1:38. *Teacher:* Now let's all close our eyes and whisper to ourselves. Softly! Say, "I'm a nice person most of the time." Say, "I'm okay!" Say it in a whisper. When you open your eyes, speech will be over. Then we'll start reading about Dick and Jane's adventures on their grandfather's farm."

**SPEECH IMPROVEMENT GOALS**

The above description of a typical speech improvement class may not do justice to the basic aims of such a project. What the teacher is attempting to do is to achieve some progress in attaining these goals:

1. To help the child identify and recognize the characteristics of the isolated speech sounds, a goal which pays dividends

not only in terms of better speech but in improving other basic skills needed in school, and to help the child explore the geography of the mouth and to improve the coördinations required for adult speech.

2. To improve the child's self-hearing and vocal phonics so that he can not only learn new pronunciations easily but also through analysis and synthesis training come to attain the phonic skills necessary in reading and spelling.

3. To improve his fluency and to resist influences tending to disrupt fluency.

4. To improve his ability to think upon his feet by training in self-talk, in commenting aloud on that which he perceives, does, or feels.

5. To create a consciousness of good voice quality as a basic asset, and to assist the child in learning how to project and monitor the intensity of his voice.

6. To help the child express his conflicts and feelings through training in speech hygiene.

Not all of these goals are touched upon at each speech improvement period, but all of them receive appropriate attention as week follows week. Individual weaknesses are protected by the group response, and at the same time the stimulus provided by the other children (with whom any single child can easily identify himself) becomes so powerful that a child tends to be pulled into conformity with the rest of the group. The whole process provides a welcome catharsis for those elementary children who find the rigors of even a modern schoolroom difficult to tolerate. Classroom teachers report that in the periods following these sessions children show increased efficiency in their other school activity and a diminution of their emotional responses.

## AN EXAMPLE OF A CORRELATED SPEECH
## IMPROVEMENT CLASS

Most classroom teachers use speech improvement periods to emphasize salient points of other projects being carried out concurrently by the class. Here is a portion of a speech improvement period as taught by a third-grade teacher whose class had been studying electricity:

1:10.   (Identifying the individual speech sounds)

*Teacher:* See this doorbell battery? Now I'm going to fasten this wire to one pole of the battery. Now I'm tapping the light bulb to the other end of the wire. But I don't have any more wire and I want to make the light come on. How can I do it? (One member of the class tells her to put the base of the bulb on the other battery connection.) All right, let's try that. (As she does so, the bulb lights up.) Now, let's see if you can tell me what sound you make turns on the light bulb. Everybody say this sentence together: "The electricity must make a complete circle!" Say it slowly and all together. (She turns on the light for the *s* sounds in the sentence, and they successfully guess the signal sound. She then points out the circuit.)

1:14.   (Vocal phonics)

*Teacher:* Here are some names of the things that need electricity to work them. Don't guess till I ring the doorbell. Ready? *k – – – ah – – r – – – z* (Bell rings, and they guess.) *Tel – uh – – gra – – ffff. T – – oh – – sss – – t – – errrrr.* Fine! You're good guessers. Now can you guess some more if I only give you a piece of the word? Here we go, and wait for the bell: *vizh.* . . . Yes, it's television. Now try this one: *ä – kyou.* . . . That's a hard one. It's *vacuum* cleaner. That runs by electricity, too, doesn't it? Here's one last one: *ä – deee.* . . . Yes, radio.

1:20. (Correcting mispronunciation)

*Teacher:* There are a lot of words about electricity which some people do not pronounce correctly. I'm going to tell you a little bit about a visit our class made last year to the radio station, but I'll say some of the words wrongly. Try to catch me and correct me. (She gives her account and makes the following errors, which some of the children catch and all correct: micaphone, bodcast, thpeaker, wadio, ehyul [aerial], and twansmitter.)

1:24. (Improving tongue coördinations)

*Teacher:* Remember what we read about Samuel Morse, the inventor of the telegraph and his Morse code? I'm going to teach you how to telegraph with your tongue. Here's the code for the word "no." (– . – – –) It is dash, dot, dash, dash, dash. But we will lift our tongues high with our mouth wide open for the dash, and stick our tongues flat for the dot. That way we can say "no" without anyone hearing us. Ready, let's go. Slow at first, then faster.

## SPEECH IMPROVEMENT AND ACADEMIC SKILLS

Speech improvement can serve as a strong reinforcer of learning skills in all other areas. Verbalization always helps the mastery of skill in the early stages. Most insights gained by children need some verbal expression to make them useful.

Here is an example of how a second-grade teacher used the speech improvement period to help her children in mastering subtraction:

1:15. (Good vocal intensity control)

*Teacher:* Remember this morning we were studying take-away in our number workbooks. This afternoon we'll use the same numbers in the same way, but we'll play take-away with our voices as well. I've written some numbers on the blackboard, and I'm going to point to them

and have you show me the answers with your vocies, like
this: The first row of children will say the first number
that I point to in a very LOUD voice. Then the second
row will say the take-away number in a very SMALL take-
away voice. Now, you people in the third row have a hard
job! You must give me the right answer in a just-right
voice—not too loud and not too soft. Let's try it now.
First row, in a very loud voice, say this number: (Teacher
points to 8 on the board.) That's good—and quite loud
too! Now, second row, in your take-away voice, say this
number (Teacher points to 4.) Now third row, give me
the right answer in a medium-sized voice. (Children respond with 4.) Good. Let's try it again with some other
numbers. (Three more subtraction problems are worked
out.) Some of the take-away voices that last time should
have been a little softer. We'll have another chance to
practice tomorrow. And we'll change rows so that everyone has a chance to practice a just-right voice.

1:20.   (Good voice quality)
*Teacher:* Now I want you to close your eyes tight and
listen hard. I'm going to the back of the room and I
want you to raise your arms when you hear a good voice,
but shake your heads when you hear a poor voice.
(Teacher illustrates a "denasal" voice by holding her
nose while saying the following sentence.) We have four
baby kittens and gave three away. How many do we have
left? (The children shake their heads.) *Teacher* (in
normal voice): That was a poor voice, wasn't it? Can
you give me the answer in a good voice? Yes, that's right,
we had one kitten left. Now close your eyes again. (This
time the teacher uses a harsh voice.) The little boy had
five pieces of candy, but the big boy took away three
pieces. (Children shake their heads again.) *Teacher:*
That was a poor voice, too. Can you imitate that voice?
The little boy has only . . . yes, two pieces of candy
left. Can you say "two" in the poor voice? All right, now

let's say "two" over again, and let's make it in a good voice.

1:24.　(Fluency improvement)

*Teacher:* I've put ten little Indians on the flannel board here. Let's have a "keep on talking" time—a time when you keep talking all the time, telling what I'm doing. For example, when I do this (teacher takes three Indians off the board), you'll say, "There are ten Indians. Teacher takes away three. There are seven Indians left." Now, I'll put the three Indians back, and we'll all do it. Remember, you must keep on talking, telling me what I'm doing with the Indians and how many are left. *Children:* There are ten Indians. Teacher takes away five. There are five Indians left. Now teacher puts back five Indians. There are ten Indians again. *Teacher:* That was right. Now, I'm going to choose someone else to be teacher. Johnny, you be our next teacher. I'll take Johnny's seat and I'll be Johnny. (Johnny has his turn, followed by three others.) That's all the time we have right now for this. There will be opportunities for the rest of you to be teachers, too, in other speech games.

1:30.　(Speech hygiene)

*Teacher:* Did you ever notice how numbers are like soldiers—soldiers who march in rows? When these soldiers stand up straight and stay in line, it's not hard to see them. But when they are sloppy and get out of line, it's hard for anyone to tell which soldier is which, and where each belongs. No matter how hard we try, the soldiers sometimes do get all mixed up. Usually we have to straighten them up if our number lesson is to make sense. Right now, though, we're going to have speech fun with the numbers. We'll get them mixed up ON PURPOSE. Take your crayons and make the soldier numbers on this big piece of drawing paper. Make the numbers any way you feel like—and while you make the numbers, let's call them by name. Look, I'll draw a big 3 like this, and while I draw it I'm going to say the number and what I think about the number . . . like, "You old three, you're so hard to draw so you look right." Remember that the numbers can be all mixed up—they don't have to be in order, or in a row, or anything. Let's even make them upside down, like this, or sideways. Let's get all the numbers through 10 helter-skelter on our page. (Pause while children draw numbers and tell what they feel about each one.) Do we all have them made? Good. Now, take a big black crayon. That'll be our ray gun and we'll use it to wipe out the soldiers. Every time you cover up a soldier with black, say, "Got you that time, you old nasty 2!" or "3" or whatever the soldier's name is. All right, turn over your sheets, and let's do it again on the other side.

## USING HOLIDAY THEMES

The speech improvement period also reflects interests of the children whenever any special holiday occurs and can be used to give release for the expression of these interests. Here is a speech improvement period reflecting the Christmas season in a first-grade room.

2:00.  (Vocal phonics)

*Teacher:* Let's have a Christmas guessing game today. I'm going to sound out some things that have to do with Christmas. Wait until I finish the word, though, because some things that start alike in the beginning have different endings. Let's see if you can guess the first one. *Sssss – – – – aaaaa – – – – nnnnn – – – – ta.* That's right, Santa. *Ch – – – iiii – – – mmmm – – – ney.* Good. Now, *sssss – – – to – – – k – – – ing* . . . stocking. On Christmas Eve, will you hate to go to *ssss – – – – lllll – – – eee – – – – p?* I thought so. But won't you be glad when you wake up in the *mmmm – – – or – – – nnnn – – ing?* Can you guess what you will find under the *trrrrr – – – – eeee?* Now I'm going to sound out some presents you might find under your tree. See if you can guess what they might be: *ssss* – – – *lllll* – – – *e* – – – – – *d* (sled); *shhhh* – – – – *oooooo* – – – – – *zzzzz* (shoes); *rrrrrr* – – – – *oh* – – – – *lllll* – – – – – *er ssssss* – – – *k* – – – *ates* (roller skates); *ka* – – – – *nnnnn* – – – *dy* (candy).

2:05.   (Correction of defective articulation)

*Teacher:* There are some words that we use a lot around Christmas time that are pretty hard to say. Would you help me work on my words today? I want you to tap your desk with your pencil when you hear a word that doesn't sound right to you. I'll stop when I hear your pencils— and then you help me to say the word right. Let's try it. Do you think it will snow on Chrithmuth? Oh! Did I make a mistake? Did you hear my mistake? Could you catch me? Yes, it should be Christmas. Would you say it with me and make the *sssss* sound very long and loud? Like this . . . Chrissssstmasssssss. I want to find a bi-cycle under the Christmas twee. . . . Yes, twee is wrong. That's right, it should be trrrrreeeee. Let's all say it. . . . Now listen. I hung up my stocking. Did you tap your pencil? I caught you that time. I didn't make a mistake that time, did I? Listen carefully because I only make a mistake sometimes. Let's try another. I want a little table and share set for Christmas. That was a mistake, wasn't it? Can you tell me what I should have said? Chair is the right way to say it, isn't it?

2:09.   (Recognition of isolated sounds)

*Teacher:* Here is a big Christmas tree on the bulletin board. And here are some Christmas tree ornaments made from paper. There's something special about these ornaments, though. They have our speech sounds that we've been learning about written on the backs of the ornaments. I'm going to hold up two of them so that all of you can see them. Now I'm going to say the sound that is written on one of them. Point to the one I'm saying. If you get it right, we'll pin it on the Christmas tree. (Teacher holds up an orange piece of paper with *sh* on it, and a red paper ball with *ch* on it.) Listen carefully . . . *shhhhhhh*. That's right, it's the orange ball. Now try this. (Teacher holds up *ch* and *rrrr*.) *Rrrrrrr*. (Teacher goes through the alphabet of sounds, presenting the children with choices such as this: *s* and *th*, *f* and *v*, *m* and *n*.)

2:15.   (Using isolated sounds in meaningful words)
*Teacher:* We have all the sounds on our tree now. Let's pretend that Christmas is over, and that Mother has said that the ornaments must be taken down and the tree taken out, since it's shedding its needles all over the rug. We're going to take it down a different way from the way we put it up, however. I'm going to point to one of the ornaments, and have you all tell me the sound. Like this. (Teacher points to purple clown, marked with *m*.) That's right. Now I'll take it off the tree as soon as someone can give me a word starting with *mmmmm*. Man? All right, I can take that one down. Now how about this one? (Teacher points to yellow *ffff*.) Is that hard? Perhaps you need a hint. Before dinner, do you have to wash your hands . . . and . . . ———— yes, *fffff*ace. F*fff*ace has the *f* sound right in the beginning, doesn't it? (Teacher completes the game, taking down all the ornaments after a word has been suggested.)

2:22.   (Coördination of the speech musculature)
*Teacher:* Let's pretend that our tongue is a Christmas tree. Make the tree stand straight and tall with the top of the tree touching the ceiling. (Place tongue with tip behind front teeth, mouth open.) The tree has very wide branches and its sides touch the sides of the room, like this. (Tongue pushes out sides of cheek—first left, then right.) To hang the lights on the tree, we go round and

round it. (Tongue is outside mouth and makes a circle, following the lip lines.) I'll have to get up on a ladder to put the angel on the top of the tree. Watch me go up and down. (Tongue moves rapidly up and down.) That's right, let's do it again; only this time let's have our tongues touch our noses. Can anyone do that? Let's put our tongue trees away for today. . . . We have to finish making the presents for Mother and Father.

## IV
### *The Alphabet of Sound*

**THE PHONETIC ALPHABET**

tu ətʃiv ækjurɪt pronʌnsɪeʃən wi mʌst lɜ˞n ðɪ ælfəbet əv saʊnd

The above sentence is written using a different alphabet from the one which we ordinarily employ. It is the International Phonetic Alphabet, with the symbols devised so that each represents one sound and one sound only. It is used throughout the world by scholars interested in recording pronunciation of both strange and familiar languages, by speech therapists, by actors and newscasters. Modern dictionaries are using it. This is what the sentence written in the phonetic alphabet says: "To achieve accurate pronunciation we must learn the alphabet of sound."

The phonetic alphabet looks strange to us, and although a few early elementary textbooks for children have been written using these strange symbols, we certainly do not recommend placing such a burden upon our children. Yet every child does learn an alphabet of sounds which is quite distinct from his reading and writing alphabet. If he is ever to learn to say the number "six" he must learn to recognize that this word contains two s sounds, one which begins it and the other which ends it. The letter x in this word represents two distinct sounds, a *k* followed by an *s*. "Sicks" and "six" are indistinguishable to the ear. In the word "exam" the *x* represents a *gz* combination. These examples are evidence of the fact that two alphabets exist, an alphabet of letters and an alphabet of sounds. There are twenty-six letters in our written English alphabet and more than forty different sounds used in spoken English. The child must master every one of these sounds if he is not to have a speech defect, to saying nothing of good speech.

## LEARNING PHONETIC SOUNDS

Any elementary teacher knows that spelling and reading require long and careful learning experience before adequate skill in using our written alphabet is gained. A similar process is required for the alphabet of sound, but since most of this learning take place prior to entrance in school, few teachers appreciate its importance. Parents, who should know better, somehow just expect the child to learn to talk correctly. They fail to give their children sufficient stimulation with isolated speech sounds to make discrimination easy. Most of us do learn to pronounce our speech sounds correctly, but we manage in spite of the poor pedagogy we receive.

When children enter school, most of them still retain some errors of substitution, omission, or distortion. We usually pay little attention to these errors, expecting that in a few years they will have disappeared. What we do not realize is that the pronunciation of strange words or names will often give us trouble unless the alphabet of sounds is mastered well and early. We do not realize that many of our problems in reading and writing and spelling stem directly from our failure to recognize that the mastery of the alphabet of letters is extremely difficult unless we have previously conquered the alphabet of sounds. Confusions in the latter will always be reflected in the former.

**PRESCHOOL SPEECH**

If you will observe a three- or four-year-old talking to himself while completely engrossed in some activity, you will notice that his mouth plays with a hundred sounds. Earlier, in his infancy, he gurgled and cooed and practiced them automatically, producing sounds used in Eskimo and in Hottentot alike. Later he will be producing the sounds of fire sirens, trains, machine guns, and rocket ships. Most adults fail to realize that this intense activity has a real utility. It is the child's way of mastering his alphabet of sounds.

Babies who are ill for much of their first years and who spend their days and nights in crying usually have articulation defects merely because they have not had sufficient practice. Anyone who has attempted to master a foreign language can testify to the need for repeated practice of the isolated sounds before he can speak the new tongue even tolerably. These sounds are learned. They are not automatically acquired. Unfortunately, many children need better teaching than they can get from this vocal play. How can a child correct a defective *r* sound if he has heard it only briefly in the swift flow of a thousand syllables? In the word "radio" the sound has a duration of less than a tenth of a second. This quick flash of sound is hardly sufficient for a small child to remember and fix in his consciousness. To him the word is a chunk of sound, a single sound. We should not wonder that he finds pronunciation difficult. How can he replace a defective sound with a correct one when he has had so little acquaintance with the latter? Adults who correct him seldom do more than say the word as a whole without ever identifying the part which is wrong. Nor do they provide him with sufficient stimulation, identification, or discrimination prac-tice on the isolated sound to help him help himself. Our children learn to speak the king's English in spite of their teachers, not because of them. And far too many never do learn to speak clearly.

## SPEECH STANDARDS

The class recitations, the oral reports, the formal announce-ments made by many high-school students are evidence of this lack of training. Few of them speak clearly. They mum-ble, slur, run words together, elide sounds and syllables, and in general manifest a grade of sloppy speech which would be intolerable if we heard it in our teachers, our radio per-sonalities, or our television idols. We tend to attribute this general unintelligibility of utterance to embarrassment or carelessness, but often the speaker just does not know how to speak any better. He has no awareness of how he sounds. He is listening to his thoughts rather than to his words. How unpleasantly surprised most of us are when first we hear our voices recorded! The foundation skill of clear speech is ability to speak individual sounds with precision and awareness of indistinctness and distortion when it does occur. Again, the trail leads us back to the need for early speech training, and to a more efficient teaching of our alphabet of sounds.

## WHEN SHOULD THE ALPHABET OF SOUND BE TAUGHT?

The majority of speech therapists feel that teaching the alphabet of sound should begin in the kindergarten and be concentrated in the first two or three grades. At this age children have the greatest motivation and interest in sounds and are most imitative. If such training is postponed until later childhood, habits of pronunciation may well have become fixed. Then, too, these are the years when children are beginning to recognize words and parts of words, when they are becoming interested in reading, writing, and spelling. The increasing interest in phonics among teachers of reading shows how important a foundation of identifiable sounds must be. A. S. Artley[1] and G. Reid[2] have provided us with careful research projects showing that speech training, much of it concentrated on the teaching of the alphabet of sound, has a marked effect in improving reading achievement. The effect of such training upon spelling achievement is undoubtedly even greater, since the first basic skill in spelling is the realization that words are composed of individual letters, many of which are truly representative of the phonetic sounds.

## HOW SHOULD THE ALPHABET OF SOUND BE TAUGHT?

In the mastery of the pronunciation of a given sound, three principles are involved: stimulation, discrimination, and identification. The first of these, stimulation, requires that the child's ears and mind become saturated with the sound, that it be prolonged or repeated long enough to serve as a vivid stimulus. Instead of requiring the child to factor out a tiny fraction of a word, the teacher presents him with the

[1] A. S. Artley, "Oral Language Growth and Reading Ability," *Elementary School Journal*, Vol. 53, 1953, pp. 321–327.

[2] Gladys Reid, "Efficacy of Speech Re-education of Functional Articulatory Difficulties in the Elementary School," *Journal of Speech Disorders*, Vol. 12, 1947, pp. 301–313.

sound itself, isolated, and vivid enough to hold all of his attention. Speech therapists working with a difficult case often "soak" the person in a veritable bath of the sound. They may have him listen for many minutes to a recording which presents the sound with different durations, or degrees of loudness, or in a different rhythmic pattern. After this bombardment, they then begin to teach him to modify his mouth and tongue appropriately to produce it. No such intensive methods are required for the normal child. About all he needs is enough stimulation to help him perceive it clearly. But he does need this!

Secondly, the child must learn the identity of each sound. As any hard-of-hearing person knows, each sound has a face to which it belongs. There are distinctive cues which can be used to translate the mouth postures into silent speech. The lips are held differently; the tongue may be lifted or protruded or grooved; the teeth may be close together or far apart; the jaw may pull down to terminate the sound. No normal child need learn to read lips, but he can often remember a given sound by remembering the facial postures which go with it. We can also help children identify a sound by calling their attention to its acoustic features. The *s* has a much higher whistling sound than does the *sh*. The *ch* is a combination of a *t* plus an *sh*, as they will readily discover if they try to alternate the words "it" and "she" at fast speech; before they know it, they are saying "itchy."

We can also help children identify the sound by calling attention to the way it is made, to its feel, to its placement. Thus, we can show a child that a *k* sound requires that the tongue-tip anchor itself against the base of the lower teeth, while in the *t* the upper teeth or upper gum is the point of contact. Children are fascinated by the geography of the mouth. They love to explore themselves.

Finally, we can help a child learn his alphabet of sounds by identifying the sound with another sound produced by something else. Thus, the *rrrrr* sound can be remembered as the sound of a growling dog; *sssss* as the air going into a tire at the filling station; *sh* as the suds going down the kitchen sink drain, or other similes which will readily call the sound to his attention. Most sounds can also be identified with a printed symbol. All of these letters are fairly phonetic and generally represent the sound: *p, t, k, b, d, g, w, m, n, f, v, z, l,* and *r*. It helps a child to realize that the sound made by biting his lower lip and then blowing is a sound represented by the symbol *f*.

Thirdly, we must help the child discriminate one sound from others which are similar to it. There are college students who have never realized that there was a difference in the pronunciations of "which" and "witch," or that we have two *th* sounds, one voiced as in "then" and the other whispered as in "think." To the Occidental all Chinese seem to look alike at first, and only as we become acquainted with individuals do we distinguish one from another. The same process is true of the speech sounds. We must live with them and play with them before they become distinct, one from another. As part of his training in the alphabet of sound, then, the child should be given the opportunity to compare one sound with another, to match a given sound against a series of assorted ones, to signal when a varying sound provided by the teacher approaches the standard, to select from a series of sounds the ones being taught. Many of these sounds must be presented along with the common errors so that discrimination can become an accomplished fact. If every first-grade teacher were to lisp *on purpose* just once a day and ask the children to catch her and correct her, the number of children who lisp would rapidly diminish.

The teaching of the alphabet of sound can be fun. Children enjoy sound play. After all, they are not far away from the long periods of babbling of their infancy. Kindergartners and first-graders are particularly intrigued by speech "play." The twisting of the tongue around new sounds and the fascination of self-hearing have a strong appeal. Since most of this speech teaching is done as a group activity, it tends to integrate a class. Teachers of this age level find it particularly helpful since much of their time is spent in helping children to conform to group behavior. In a speech play period the shy child is protected by his anonymity. The good speaker helps the poorer. Tensions disappear. And great profit results in terms of all the language skills.

## PRESENTING THE ALPHABET OF SOUND

An elementary teacher may readily conceive of the benefit her children would derive from presentation of the alphabet of sound but find it difficult to see how such activity might be planned and carried out. One teacher reported:

Sure, I can see that learning an alphabet of sounds would help the children in my room in their speech, and in their reading and spelling as well. It seems like a good idea. . . . But where do I begin? I'm no speech therapist. Terms like stimulation, discrimination, and identification of sounds are meaningless to me right now. Oh, I know how to define them . . . but not really how to use them. I don't know how to plan speech activities that would incorporate them. Please tell me just *how* you start. How should I go about presenting the alphabet of sound?

Teaching the alphabet of sound is not so different from teaching reading or spelling. The reading program starts with reading readiness and preprimers, the study of arithmetic with the simple counting of objects. Just as in the teaching of reading or numbers, there is a general outline which may be followed in presenting the alphabet of sound.

In planning such an outline, the task will not seem so great when we remember that it is not necessary or even wise to present every speech sound in our language. Instead, we will concentrate only on the consonant sounds which are used most frequently in our language and those which are most commonly misarticulated. Some speech errors are more easily discernible than others. If a child substitutes or omits an *sssss* sound consistently, his teacher will be quick to discover the error. However, if he has the same kind of difficulty with a *th* or a *y* sound, the error may not be immediately apparent.

Speech therapists have discovered that most of their work with children having articulatory errors is likely to center around eight consonant sounds: *r, s, l, sh, k, th, ch,* and *f.* Of these, four present the most difficulty to early elementary children: *r, s, l,* and *th*. With these facts in mind, we will outline our program in speech improvement so that when presenting our speech alphabet the emphasis will be placed on these sounds. The sounds which cause the most difficulty will need the most attention. The four most difficult sounds (*r, s, l, th*) will need a series of lessons, while the other consonant sounds may need only one or two sessions.

Each sound presented to the children should become a distinct personality with a distinguishable character of its own. Each sound must have its own face, its own gestures, its own name and personality. It should radiate its own visual and auditory impression. By use of all these cues, it becomes a separate and distinct entity, a "person" with a special role to play in speech.

During the process of identifying speech sounds, the geography of the mouth is explored, bit by bit. Having the children make the sound *silently* is an excellent way of introducing them to the placement of the mouth, tongue, teeth, or lips for that particular sound. The geography of the mouth can be further explored by tongue gymnastics. Children are invariably delighted with "tongue tales" of various kinds. These stories, told by the teacher, require the children to follow along and supply all actions and sound effects through tongue movements. Many teachers are familiar with the story of Mrs. Tongue, who spends most of her time cleaning her house (the mouth). This energetic and industrious woman even sweeps the ceiling (the palate), the walls (sides of the mouth), the stairways (teeth), and shakes her broom (the tongue) with vigor outside her home. She then looks on the roof for her lost kitten (tongue pointed toward nose) and in the basement (tongue pointed toward chin). After taking one last "peek" (grooving of tongue) for her lost cat, she retires into her home and shuts the door (lips).

The tongue, versatile as it is, can be a merry-go-round, a telephone pole, a slide, a pinwheel. It can hump and point and click and curl. By its use, the children can discover all the hills, valleys, and ridges inside their mouths, both in silence and in the production of sounds. The tongue movement which belongs with each speech sound can be stressed, along with the other parts of the speech apparatus which might be used.

Thus children learn to identify a sound not only by its visual and auditory clues but by its placement as well. Identification and recognition of each sound should be sought through all these channels. Children will soon learn to recall a sound through any one of its various cues. They will be able to remember a sound by the name of the sound alone, by the gesture associated with that sound, or by the position of the lips and tongue as the sound is seen but not heard. They will be able to interrelate all these factors with the auditory impression of the sound.

In order to obtain such identification of the various sounds, the children as a group must be interested in learning these sound characteristics. Drill on sounds alone will not produce any such sustained interest. What will?

First of all, each sound is presented separately. It is given a name. This name not only distinguishes the particular sound from all others in the alphabet of sounds but also hints at some other characteristic of the sound. It may be an auditory characteristic, such as calling the *ssss* sound Timmy Teakettle or Sammy Snake. It may be a visual characteristic, such as a finger raised to the lips for the "be quiet" sound, *shhhhh*. It may be a tactile sensation, such as holding the hand to the larynx to feel the vibration when a *zzzzz* is produced. All of these methods may be used to aid in the identification of a single sound.

For example, a second-grade teacher introduced the *sssss* sound this way:

I'd like to have everyone close his eyes tight and listen very carefully. I'm going to make a sound, and I want you to guess what it is. Now keep your eyes closed until I ask you to open them and listen to this: *sssss ss sssss s sssss sssss ss sssssss*. Now open your eyes and tell me what it sounded like to you. A flat tire? Yes, it could be that. An angry cat? Perhaps. A hissing snake? Why, yes. A giraffe? I don't think a giraffe makes any noise at all, does he? A teakettle on the stove? Yes, that's an especially good one. Let's name this sound—the *ssss* sound— the teakettle sound, shall we? Now watch my mouth as I make the sound for you . . . *sssssss*. See how my teeth are together! I'm very careful not to let my tongue peek at all. Let's all make the teakettle sound together now . . . I'll drop this feather and we'll all say *sssss* as long as it floats in the air. When it touches the floor, everybody stop. Here we go . . . *sssssssssss* . . . good! Let's try it again, and be very sure your tongue is behind your teeth and does not peek out.

The teacher also introduced some visual material as she used the *s* sound. On the board she sketched many of the things the children had mentioned, a flat tire, a teakettle, a snake. Under each one of these sketches she drew the letter *s*. She had the children pretend to be each of these things, always identifying the sound with the letter written beneath the drawing. Thus she linked the alphabet and the visual and acoustic qualities of the *s* sound.

After each sound is presented individually, the children should be given the opportunity of identifying the sound in words.

Do you all remember the teakettle sound? It's *sssssss*. That's right. Now I'm going to give you some words, and when you hear the teakettle sound, clap your hands. Here's the first word . . . *ssssss*wing. Did you all hear the *ssss* sound? Good . . . now listen closely and see if you can catch the sound. Yes*sssss*. Some of you heard the sound even though it came at the end of the word, "yes." Here's another word . . . "ball." No teakettle sound in that word. Let's try one more word . . . "ice cream" (*isssss* cream). You all clapped that time. I'm glad you heard the teakettle sound. It came in the middle of the word that time. Listen to that word again . . . *isssss* cream. Hear it in the middle? Next time we'll play a game called "Where's My Sound?" and you can help me find the teakettle sound, whether he's in the beginning, the middle, or hiding at the end of a word. Meanwhile, be looking for the *ssss* sound when you are listening to each other in our reading groups. How many of you will remember what the teakettle sound is like?

Next the teacher helps the children discriminate between the *s* sound and other sounds commonly substituted for it, such as the *th*, the *t*, or the *sh*. Here is an example of a discrimination game:

All of us make mistakes with our words and our sounds at one time or another. Today I'd like you to help me catch my mistakes. Would you all raise your hand when you hear me make a mistake? Let's see how many of you can catch me! "I don't like to wash with *thoap* and water." I made a mistake on one word. Do you know which one it was? You raised your hand, Johnny— you caught me. Can you show me the right way to say that word? *Sssss*-oap. That sounds much better, doesn't it. *Sssssssoap*. Thank you, Johnny. Oh, I just now remembered! I let my tongue peek between my teeth—and I mustn't do that if I want a good teakettle sound. Would you ALL help me remember by saying *sssssoap* with your teeth together and a good strong *sssss* right at the beginning. Thank you. I'll try not to make that mistake again. Let's try another sentence: "I like to watch *Shpace* Cadets on television every Friday." I see most of your hands up. Now this time, let me see if I can find my own mistake and correct it by myself. Will you clap your hands when I get it right? Let me try now . . . *shpace* . . . no, that's too sloppy and slushy . . . *thpace* . . . no, that's like a baby—I forget to keep my tongue behind my teeth . . . pace . . . oh, no, I forgot the *sssss* entirely that time. *Sssssspace* . . . there, that's it . . . *ssspace* cadets! And you all clapped.

## GROUP RESPONSE

Many of the speech activities suggested for presenting the alphabet of sound require a speech response from the classroom as a whole. Of necessity, such unison activity is controlled activity if the children are to benefit from participation in group speech response. A strong, accurate response by the group helps to vivify the response for each child in the group. Those who are unable to produce a sound correctly are able to approach a more adequate articulation through this strong stimulation. The effect is much like that derived from singing in a chorus. Average voices are strengthened by the addition of superior voices, since the average singer hears not only himself but the other voices almost as if they were his own. Self-hearing is supplemented and the speech response is improved by the strong stimulation provided.

A choirmaster has a group of disciplined performers; the first- or second-grade teacher does not, nor does she need to demand that type of perfection. However, indirect control over the speech responses of the children is necessary. This control may be accomplished by limiting the response. For example:

We'll all say *shhhh* to the doll in the cradle because she's crying. We start as the cradle starts rocking and when it stops, we'll all stop.

*or*

I borrowed this yo-yo from Lynn. I'm going to try to make it go "round-the-world." You can help me by making the *rrrrr* sound whenever the yo-yo is in the air. When it's in my hand, everyone is to say *aaaaaaay.* Let's try it now . . . remember to alternate *rrrrr–aaaaaay–rrrrrrrr–aaaaaaay.* Let's start . . . *rrrrrrr–aaaa, rrrrrr–aaaa. Rrray.* Listen . . . we made a word with those two sounds . . . *Rr-ay.* Anyone guess what word it is? It's someone's name. Everyone who thinks he knows point to that person!

Such definite limits on the children's responses are valuable in keeping their verbal velocity under control. There will be other times, in other phases of speech improvement, when no such definite control is established. In presenting the alphabet of sounds, however, the teacher is interested in maintaining a unison speech response to a large degree.

Such unison verbal response can be complemented by unison physical activity. The activity can serve a double purpose. It can be directly related to the sound being introduced and it can relieve the tension which comes from listening intently.

We have learned about several sounds and now we're ready to play the train game. Will you all line up, with your hands on the shoulders of the person in front of you? Good. Now, Barbara, you're the engine. You'll steer the train around the room on its track. Remember, the train starts with a slow *ch—ch—ch*, and then goes faster and faster. All right . . . *ch—ch—ch—ch, ch–ch–ch–ch.* . . . Now, raise your hands and pull the train whistle —*sssssssss, sssssssss.* Slow the train down, *ch–ch–ch–ch—ch——ch.* . . . Let the steam out . . . *shhhhhhh, shhhhhh,* and the train comes to a stop!!

Do you remember how hard it rained on Tuesday? The wind was blowing, too, and it made the trees bend and sway. Let's all stand up and bend the way the trees did, and make the sound of the wind swishing the branches around. Our arms can be the branches of the tree. Here's the sound of the rain and the wind . . . *shhhhhh, shhhhhh.*

Teachers who have experimented with speech improvement find that a frequent shift of activities helps to maintain the interest of the children and to keep them alert and listening. This need not mean shifting the focal point of interest, however. As a number of searchlights might play on a theater marquee, so may the teacher provide a number of activities revolving around a single sound. Tongue exercises, vocal phonics, and various discrimination games can all stress a single sound and the movements necessary to enunciate that sound. If, for example, the children were working on the *llll* sound, tongue games that day might be something like this:

You remember that in making the L sound, we must put the tip of our tongues up, like this, *la, la.* I want you to pretend that your tongues are telephone poles . . . make them stand straight up in your mouth. Watch mine! Now they'll be talking telephone poles. Draw them down quickly. Make the pole say, *lee— lai—low—loo.*

How many of you can make your tongues touch your nose? Let's try to make them touch our noses first, and then our chins . . . up, down, up, down. Good. Sally is able to touch her nose. And Jerry, you can touch your chin, can't you?

## HOW TO MAKE THE MOST COMMONLY DEFECTIVE SOUNDS

To aid children in distinguishing between the various sounds in the speech alphabet, teachers use the cues that have been previously suggested. They identify the sound with another kind of sound, a sound that is already familiar to the child. The placement approach is combined with this, and the child is asked to identify the sound not only by its name but also by the position of the lips, teeth, and tongue required for that sound. Then, too, almost every sound is also defined through a characteristic and symbolic gesture, as when the finger is raised to the lips to go with *shhhh.*

Here are some illustrations of how the most commonly

defective sounds might be presented and how to help the children make the sound correctly:

s sound

You've met the teakettle sound before. Remember? It's a sharp, whistling sound, like this: sssssssss, sssssss. This is how we make it: Put your teeth together and blow . . . ssssss. Try it. Fine. Now when you make the sound I want you all to pretend you are teakettles, too, and that you're going to catch the sound

The Teakettle Sound.

as it comes out the spout of the teakettle and draw it out. Put your fingers to your lips and draw the sound out . . . way out . . . sssssss. Just the way steam comes out of the teakettle on the stove.

Sometimes if we aren't careful, the sssss sound may become sloppy and slushy, just as if you were eating mashed potatoes as you talked. When this happens, try to make a good ssss sound by putting your tongue behind your *upper* teeth and then blowing. If you remember to keep your teeth together your sssss will be a clear, whistling sound. Keeping your teeth together is pretty important, though. You can't make a good teakettle sound without it. If your tongue peeks between your teeth, you may have a *th* sound, which isn't the same thing at all.

Here's a picture of Timmy Teakettle. I'm going to put him on the chalk rail at the end of the blackboard. Every time we all make a good *sssss* sound, Timmy will do a somersault, down the chalk rail. Let's make Timmy somersault all the way down to the other end of the rail. Let's have each row take turns in making Timmy somersault. . . . *sssss, sssssss, sssssss, sssssss.*

### er sound

Today we're going to meet another sound. This new sound is the fire engine sound. I want you to close your eyes and listen to the siren wailing as the fire engine rushes to a fire . . . *errrrrrrrrr.* Hear how the siren sounds. Now watch my hand as I make the sound. My hand goes up when the siren sounds higher, and goes down when the siren wails lower.

errrrr<sup>rr</sup>rrrrrrrrr<sub>rrrr</sub>rr<sub>rrrrrrr</sub>

Let's all be a fire engine now, and make a good *errrr* sound. That was a good long siren sound and I'm sure every car got out of the way. Now I want you to practice short siren sounds with me, like this: *er, er, er.*

The fire engine sound is sometimes hard to make. That may be because you're keeping your tongue tip down. Let's keep the tip of our tongue up and smile as we make a short fire engine sound, *er, er, er.* When we smile, it draws our lips back and helps us make a good *er.*

Here's a picture of Fergie, the fire engine. And here's a little

Fergie, the Fire Engine.

red plastic engine that looks like the picture of Fergie. I'm going to shove it across the floor. While it's moving I want you to make the fire engine sound, but the minute it stops when it hits the wall, everyone stop saying *errrr*. All right, here we go . . . *errrrrr*.

*k* sound

We call the *kuh* sound the coughing sound. Let's put our

Kiki, the Crow.

hand to our mouth so we can feel the sound as it comes out . . . *kuh, kuh, kuh.* Can you feel the air on your hand? It's hard to see how to make a *kuh,* because we make it with the back of our tongues against the back of our mouths. But you can feel the coughing sound. Put your hand on your throat and see if you can feel your voice box wiggle as you say *kuh.* Good. Be sure the tip of your tongue is anchored behind your lower teeth. We want the front part of our tongue to rest while the back of the tongue does all the work for this sound. Let's try it together now, *kuh . . . kuh.*

Remember that when you make the coughing sound, you always put your hand up to cover your mouth, just as if you really had a cold or something were caught in your throat.

Here's a picture of Kiki, the old black crow. He stole some corn out of the farmer's field and now the corn is stuck in his throat and he's coughing and crying, "kaw, kaw." I'll pretend to be Kiki, and every time I put my claw to my throat, you help me spit out the corn by saying *kuh, kuh.*

*lllll* sound

Here's another sound to add to our alphabet of sound. It's called the peanut butter sound sometimes because we can pretend we're wiping peanut butter off the roof of our mouths. Let's open our mouths wide, like this, and then make our tongues stand straight up like a telephone pole until the tip touches the roof of our mouth right behind our teeth. Explore with the tip of your tongue. Can you feel the little ridge, or rough part, that's right behind your front teeth? Let's pretend we've had a picnic and have eaten a peanut butter sandwich. We want to get the peanut butter off the roof of our mouth. We'll wipe it off quickly, like this . . . *la, la, la.* I'm going to make my finger do what my tongue does. Watch! First I raise it straight up and then bring it forward and down quickly . . . *la, la.*

Sometimes people have trouble making a good peanut butter sound because their tongue won't go up by itself. If you're having trouble, try this: Let's all open our mouths and then hang on to our jaws with our right hand . . . don't let your jaw wiggle now. Make it stay still and have your tongue do all the work.

Here's a picture of a little boy eating peanut butter. Mary, please come and stand beside me. . . . Now every time you touch the picture, everyone has to make the peanut butter sound. Let's see if you can touch it and make us say *la* just as if we were singing "Jingle Bells.". . . *la, la, la . . . la, la, la . . . la, la, la, la, la.*

*th* sound

I've drawn a funny face on the blackboard . . . and you can see that he's sticking his tongue out at us. In just a moment, we're going to stick out our tongues at him and make his sound. Listen carefully to hear it . . . you stick out your tongue and blow, like this . . . *th, th, th.* That's Mr. Tattle Tongue. Let's all say *th* to his silly face. Be sure you blow air when you say

Lll, the Peanut Butter Sound.

his sound. Look how far out *his* tongue is. Can you get your tongue that far out in making his sound?

Mr. Tattle Tongue has a very long tongue and he sticks it way out. That's because so many of us forget to put our tongues way out between our teeth. When we forget we're likely to say things like "*f*um" instead of "*th*umb." Mr. Tattle Tongue knows that we aren't even using his sound when we do things like that.

You've seen lots of boys and girls make a silly face like this— they stick out their tongues and waggle their fingers near their ears. Let's see if you can do that now as you make the Tattle Tongue sound. I have a picture here of Mr. Tattle Tongue . . . see how his tongue moves in and out of the little slot? Whenever you see his tongue come out, you make the same funny face and say *th.*

*ch* sound

I know that you've all heard trains chugging by on the railroad tracks. We have a speech sound that is just like a train going fast. Listen . . . *ch, ch, ch, ch.* Bring your tongue up

Th, the Tattle Tongue Sound.

to the roof of your mouth, just as if you were going to say *t*. Now bring it down quickly and say *ch, ch*.

Let's pretend our hands are those rods on the great big wheels of the train. You've seen them move back and forth like this as the wheels turn around. First our right hand goes forward, and then as it comes back, our left goes forward. Each time we'll say *choo, choo*. Let's make the train go very, very slowly at first—a slow-motion train. Now we'll make our hands go faster and the train sound will go faster, too. Make sure

The Train Sound.

that when you say the train sound, it's *ch, ch, choo*. Sometimes people say *shoe*—and that's something you wear on your feet, not something you can take a trip on, like a train. Here's a picture of our train sound. I'll hold it so you can all see it. Now, every time I tap my foot, I want you to make the sound. Listen carefully because this tapping will go fast, go slow, and go fast again.

*f* sound

Do you have a kitten at your house? I'll bet one of your friends has one, even if there isn't one at your house. The sound we're going to learn about today is the one that sounds like a very angry cat . . . *fffffffff*. We'll call this sound the spitting

The Kitty Sound.

cat sound. Listen to it and you'll be able to picture a kitten who is very mad, scratching with his tiny claws and saying *fffffff*. He's probably trying to pretend that he's like some big cat—a lion, or a tiger.

When you make the sound, be sure to bite your lower lip and blow through your teeth. Let's try it together, *ffffff, ffff, ffff*. Now let's put our finger right below our lips, so that we can feel the air come out. Say *fffffff*, and feel the air on your finger.

Here's a picture of our angry kitten. I'm going to walk around the class now. You all close your eyes. I want everyone to be ready to say the *fffff* sound. Get your teeth on the lower lip and be all set to make

the sound. Then when you feel this picture of the kitten touch you on your head, you make the sound. No one will know just when he'll feel the kitten, so you must all be ready all the time.

*sh* sound

When you want to tell someone else to keep quiet, what

sound do you use? *Shhhhhh* is a good way of saying "keep quiet," isn't it? When anyone hears that, he knows that it means to be still. In fact, lots of times your mother has only to put her finger warningly to her lips, like this, and you know that you are supposed to be still. I often ask you to be quiet, but now it's YOUR turn to tell me to be quiet by saying *shhhhhh*. All of you raise your fingers to your lips and say *shhhh* whenever I put my head down. All right, here we go . . . *shhhhh, shhhhh, shhhh, shhhhhh.*

The *Be Quiet* Sound.

Remember that the *shhhh* sound is not a loud sound, but a low, quiet sound. You make the "keep quiet" sound by keeping your teeth together, just as you did for the teakettle sound, but this time, you don't need a high whistling sound like *s*, but instead you want others to move softly and speak very quietly, so you need a soft, quiet *shhhh*.

Let's pretend we're watching Roy Rogers on television and your baby brother is making too much noise. We're going to tell him to be still every time he shouts, "Giddyap." I'll be the little boy, and you tell me *shhhhh*.

In the above illustrations an attempt has been made to introduce each sound in such a manner that it can be identified with a noise or sound that is likely to be perceived in the children's own environment. Once a sound has been given a name, it is wise to use this name thereafter. However, the above labels are only suggestions and need not be used. Many other appropriate names will occur to a teacher. If your school is heated by steam, you may possess an obliging radiator that will produce a *sssss* sound, not to mention other clanks and bangs which may not be so readily definable.

Whatever you may choose to represent the sound, this labeling procedure is further developed by associating a gesture, a visual stimulus (such as a picture), and a description of the placement of the lips, tongue, or teeth. These additional cues are extremely useful in helping children identify and discriminate between the various sounds in the speech alphabet.

## OTHER SOUNDS IN OUR ALPHABET OF SOUND

In the foregoing section we illustrated how the most commonly mispronounced sounds might be presented to a group of early elementary children. There are other sounds, of course, and they may be presented as the teacher's time, energy, and interests dictate. After these most commonly defective sounds are thoroughly understood, pairs of twin sounds (called cognates) are presented. Teachers have found that speech work on the twin sounds, where their likenesses and differences are explained, is of help when the children meet these sounds in their reading. Such cognate sounds are: *f* and *v*, *k* and *g*, *t* and *d*, *p* and *b*, and the voiced and unvoiced *th* sounds. The twin sounds might be introduced like this:

You've already met the spitting cat sound—remember the angry kitten who said *ffffff*? Now I'd like to have you meet his sound twin, a sound that's made exactly the same way, but this time, instead of blowing air while you bite your lower lip, you make a sound too. Like this: *vvvvvvv*. It sounds like an airplane, doesn't it?

Put your hand to your throat and feel the airplane's motor inside. Let's see if we can say the sound twins. First the quiet one—that's the kitten, *ffffff*. Then the noisy one, *vvvvvv*—that's the airplane sound.

Now I'm going to divide the room in halves. This half of the room will be the kitten, and this half the airplane. All you kittens get down on the floor and scratch with your claws as you make your sound. Let's see if you can do it four times, one for each paw. Good. Now the airplanes are to stand up tall and make your hands and arms be an airplane. Let's make our airplane dive four times, *vvvvv*, *vvvvv*, *vvvvvv*, *vvvvv*.

As can be seen by this illustration, sound twins, or cognates, consist of one sound which is the quiet or whispered sound and another which is described as a "noisy" sound, or a voiced sound. A very clear example of such cognates is the *sssss* sound and the *zzzz* sound. The children can feel the noisy or voiced sounds by holding their hands to their throats. The vibration of the larynx is quite noticable. Suggestions for presenting these sounds are as follows:

1. *s* and *z*: *Ssss* is the teakettle sound, while *zzzz* is the bumble-bee sound. The children can feel the buzzing of the bee in their voice box.
2. *f* and *v*: *Ffff* is the spitting cat sound; *vvvv* the airplane sound. The children can feel the vibration of the airplane motor.
3. *k* and *g*: *Kuh* is the coughing crow sound, while *guh* is the frog sound. This is a little more difficult to differentiate, since the sounds are not continuants (sounds which can be prolonged easily).
4. *t* and *d*: *Tuh* is the small drum which sounds like rat-a-tat-tat; *duh* is the big bass drum. Here again the difference may be more difficult to distinguish than in the continuants.
5. *th* and *th*: The whispered *th* is the Tattle Tongue sound; the voiced *th* is the truck sound. It is important that the tongue be protruded between the teeth for both these sounds.
6. *p* and *b*: The whispered sound is *puh* and that can be identified as the sound that blows out a match or candle; the voiced sound, *buh*, is the motorboat sound.

All twin sounds must be identified first as two distinct entities with their own individual characteristics. Then these sounds are presented together and compared, and discrimination between the two sounds is attempted. Such discrimination can be done through a series of speech games, like this one:

You'll remember that we learned about Kiki the crow and the coughing sound he made. Everyone put up your hand to your mouth and show me how you make the coughing sound. Good. Now here's a twin to our coughing sound. It's the frog sound, *guh*. That's because when you say *guh, guh*, deep in your throat, you sound just like a frog croaking in his pond. I'd like to have you listen and see if you can guess which twin is the noisy one . . . *kuh—guh* . . . *kuh—guh*. Mmmmm . . . now let's see if your guess was right. Everyone put a hand to his throat and say the sounds with me. You'll be able to tell the noisy sound by the way your throat trembles . . . *kuh—guh*. That's right, *guh*, the frog sound, is the noisy twin. The coughing sound, *kuh*, is the quiet one of the pair.

Now let's see if you can guess which sound I'm going to use.

## USING THE SOUND ALPHABET IN LATER
## ELEMENTARY GRADES

Although some people might wonder if the sound alphabet would hold any interest for the fifth- or sixth-grade child, we have found no diminishing of response among older children. Of course, the activities must be built around their more mature interests and language level, but the children in this age group also find our tongue a strange and wonderful mixture which they do not fully comprehend. Since our language often halts adults in their tracks, it is not surprising that it causes great confusion and wonderment among children. Playing with and manipulating our speech sounds is one way to help children master a partially learned and necessary skill.

Naturally, the alphabet of sound is presented with more emphasis on the relationship between oral and written communication. Once the sound alphabet has been grasped, the challenge for older children is in speed of discrimination, rapid response to sound stimuli, and increasing their ability to identify and manipulate the speech sounds in complex situations.

Good speech is built upon a firm foundation of adequately produced speech sounds. Children in the elementary school need the help of their teacher, first, in creating that foundation, and second, in building upon it a structure of adequate oral communication.

# V
# Self-Hearing
# and Vocal Phonics

## THE BUILT-IN MONITOR

In the improvement of speech, the ability to hear oneself as well as the other person is of vital importance. Although in the very young child, engaged in the process of learning his first words, this self-hearing is intense, awareness of one's own voice fades with the years. And it should do so if we are to communicate with any swiftness. Only occasionally are we forced to listen to ourselves: when we must pronounce an unfamiliar name or a strange word, or when we misspeak. This indicates that self-hearing is still present. It monitors our utterance unobtrusively, coming to consciousness only when needed.

Since our purpose is the improvement of oral communication, we must necessarily exploit this monitoring device. Those of us who have to master a foreign language, who seek to improve our singing voices, or who desire to improve in public speaking soon find that we must learn to listen to ourselves. We must be able to hear ourselves if we are to make any progress. The disbelief and surprise with which we first hear our recorded voices indicate that self-hearing is not to

Self-Hearing.

be achieved by will power alone. Training is needed. A famous voice teacher once said that nine-tenths of all her time was spent, not in teaching her pupils to sing, but in teaching them to hear the notes they were producing, and that the better they heard them, the better they sang. In speaking, much the same situation exists.

## IMPROVED MONITORING DEVICES

By itself, of course, self-hearing would have little value. We must hear ourselves in comparison to others. The northerner in Louisiana first begins to hear the odd pronunciation of his Southern friends; then he finds out that it is his own sounds that are strange, and he begins to listen comparatively. In any speech improvement process much of this matching of one's own self-heard utterance with that of a model must take place.

We must learn to scan our voices, our fluency, our pronunciation if we hope to improve them. If each of us were forced each evening to listen to a recording of everything we had spoken during the day, we would probably talk less but talk better, if indeed we could survive the experience. If you have heard secret recordings of party conversations or impromptu discussions, you will know what we mean. The speech is sloppily articulated, very broken; the voices are shrill or rasping; the thinking is often incoherent. Can we not hope for better things for our children? We must teach them to master the great tool of human speech, not merely to fumble with it amateurishly. The present state of the world requires better tools of communication and thinking than we possess if a free society is to survive. Like the soldier, our children need a basic training program so that they will not falter under stress. The heart of such a program must be the ability to scrutinize one's own attempts to communicate. This is what we are lumping together within the category of self-hearing.

The child in the early elementary grades always seems to be fascinated by himself. Of course, such self-interest hardly distinguishes him from his elders. The most interesting thing in the world is the perpendicular pronoun, I, and at any age. But the child under ten is still close to that baby who played with his toes and found the corners between his fingers one of the wonders of the world. He loves to explore himself. We adults have forgotten the wonderful mechanism of our beings. Like the grass or the stars, we take ourselves for granted. Not so with the primary child. If you help him to listen to himself, he will be delighted by the experience.

He is also much more flexible than the adult, less rigid. Just as he still mutters jargon to himself or plays with a thousand vocal noises (descendants of the early babbling), playing with sounds still retains attractiveness. He can experiment with his voice, modify his rate or rhythms, assume with surprising mimicry variable pronunciations with an ease we adults could well envy. Foreign children seem to pick up the inflection patterns and correct sounds of English much more easily and completely than foreign adults because of this flexibility and interest. Surely we should use these traits and this time for teaching better communication.

## VOCAL PHONICS

We have found that one of the quickest and best ways of getting children to hear themselves talk is through training in vocal phonics. This term refers to the ability to analyze words into their component sounds and to synthesize a series of sounds into words. Thus, the word "phone," if analyzed, is composed of three sounds—an initial *f*, a medial *o*, and a final *n* sound. Similarly, the three sounds *n*, *o*, and *z* when synthesized in that order produce the word "nose." These twin processes of analysis and synthesis must take place in any act of self-correction of a defective pronunciation. Usually they occur without much consciousness but they do occur. If a child says "wabbit" for "rabbit" he will, in overcoming this error, have to realize that the two words have different heads, even though the bodies and tails are the same. He will have to locate the error in the sound sequence. This involves analysis. Also, he will have to replace his beginning errored sound with a new and more acceptable one, the *r*. This involves synthesis. Both forms of vocal phonics require the discriminative hearing of oneself and others.

It might be objected that training in self-hearing and vocal phonics may disrupt the smoothness of the child's verbal skills, or that no such analysis should be attempted so early, since it is probably beyond the child's powers. That these objections are of doubtful validity is shown by the child's own behavior. Long before he enters school he has played with words, rhyming them, dissecting them, varying them. In another book (C. Van Riper, *Teaching Your Child to Talk*), the senior author has described this normal fascination with vocal phonics in this way:

Normal children eventually learn the principles of vocal phonics, the synthesis and analysis of words, by playing with words, by rhyming, by punning, by distorting their sequences. They find great interest in comparing and contrasting words which provide a small difference in a larger similarity. They are fascinated by "fee, fie, fo, fum," by "eeny, meeny, miney, mo," by "Humpty Dumpty."

At first the child prefers exact duplication, but he passes through that stage and comes to love rhyming for its own sake. If you eavesdrop on the child playing with his toys, you will hear him practicing his vocal phonics: "Foggie, old foggie-foggie, you old goggie you, boggy, boggy, boo, boggie-bogguh." This is vocal play, but a more purposive type. Inflections abound. Word stems are isolated and different beginnings and endings are practiced. You can hear the child stressing certain parts of a well-known word: Yessssss, sssss, yesssssyesssss. Nnnnnnno you don't Nnnnnnnnno. Yesssssss, no." Sometimes they will even mutilate words which they can pronounce perfectly. We have heard children (in their private play) counting: "ton-two-tee" when they have long been able to pronounce those digits correctly.

They also have fun adding endings to familiar words, and usually they use the common *ee* ending for this purpose. First they review the familiar nursery words: "babee!" (with the second sound stressed), "daddeeeee," "kitty," "mummy" and then they try it on other words: "Dadeee has a pipeee" (gales of laughter); "puttee bookee on cherry" (convulsions); "Baddy Daddy, Baddy Daddy," "Mummy has a big tummy, has a bummy, a dummy; Mummy is a fummy." They grow weak with mirth. If punning is the lowest form of wit, it is also the earliest. Most parents fail to see not only the "humor" in these performances (and who could blame them?) but also the utility which this punning and rhyming undoubtedly have for the learning of proper pronunciation. By these activities the child learns to observe all the features of a given word. He plays with its beginning; he twists its tail.

Speech correction teachers have found that it is almost impossible to teach a child to correct his articulation errors until he has learned to listen to the words he utters and to take them apart and rearrange them. So far as we are concerned here, the most important feature of vocal phonics is not just that it facilitates the pronunciation of new words and eliminates mispronunciations but that it is especially valuable in promoting self-hearing. Many adults have difficulty in pronouncing such a word as "statistics," merely because they have never done the necessary analysis into *sta* and *tis* and *tics*. Children have similar problems in mastering new words and strange names. Rather than laugh at their errors or merely place a stronger demand for correct utterance, we should help them locate their difficulty. Vocal phonic training, then, has immediate and long-lasting practical value in the mastery of pronunciation. But as we have said, its value in helping the individual learn to listen to himself is even greater. Self-hearing helps not just the pronunciation skills but all the others. It creates a healthy intolerance for hemming and hawing, for the jumbled haphazard utterance, for the harsh or nasal voice, for the unclear thought. Any teacher who listens to the fumbling way in which much of the information volunteered during recitation is given will know that something should be done to help her students express themselves more adequately. It is tragic that we continually accept as sufficient such recitations. By that acceptance, we actually condone sloppy thinking and expression. We teach our children that it is enough. Life through its penalties will teach another lesson and offer its rewards to others who can communicate more effectively. The key to better self-expression is better self-hearing. We should not deny our children that key.

## PRESENTING VOCAL PHONICS TO THE CLASS

We have suggested that vocal phonics can help the child in self-hearing. Before we can hope to have him consciously and conscientiously use his self-hearing to improve his speech, we must present him with the opportunity to use and practice vocal phonics. How can this be done?

Vocal phonics can be practiced with the whole class, each child responding in unison with the group, each child a par-

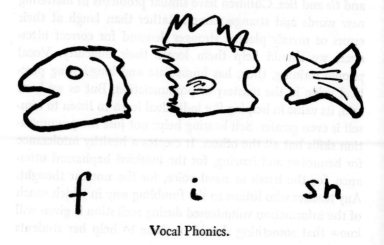

**Vocal Phonics.**

ticipant. In introducing vocal phonics, the teacher sets the stage. She is the one to take a word apart and put it back together again. For example:

We were talking the other day about words having heads, bodies, and tails. Often we look at or hear a word as a whole person, never thinking to look at its separate parts. But today we're going to practice taking words apart out loud, and then putting them together silently. Let's call this game Finger Phonics. I'll sound out an object in the room, and I'd like all of you to point to it. Now don't give it away by saying it out loud. Just point, and then I'll know you've been able to put the word together. Try this one: *lllllll – – – ai – – – – t*. Did you all point to a light? Good. Here's another one: *fffff – – – – lllllll – – – – – or*. Yes, floor is right. Here's one more: *sssss – – – – eeeee – – – lllll – – – – – ing* . . . ceiling.

Here's another sounding-out game. It's called Busy Phonics. I'm going to try to keep you all busy doing things that I sound out. Listen carefully, put the sounds together to make a word, and then do as the word says. Let's see if you can all *ssss – – mmmmm – – ai – – – lllll*. Those are certainly big smiles. Can you *ssss – – t – and*? Fine, now, *djjjjj – uuuuuu – mp!* Did you all jump? Let's see if you can *t – urrrrr – nnnnn*. Turn. Now let's all *sssss – – iiii – – tt*.

You know how mixed up a movie, or a television show, can seem if you've missed part of it. You often don't know why the people on the screen act as they do if you've missed the beginning of the show. It's just the same way when you miss the beginning of a word. But let's see if you can guess what word I'm sounding out, even though I'll leave off the first sound. _____ – – *aaaa – – – – t*. Can't anyone guess? Let's see if this will help you. Last night I went to the movies and I (appropriate action by teacher) . . . yes, sat down. That's the word, *sssss – – – aaa – t*. Here's another word with the same middle and end sounds: . . . *aaaaaa – – – – t*. When I come into the house, I wipe my feet on a _____ *aaa – t*. Rug? Oh, now, listen again. Yes, that's it, a *mmmmmm – aaa – t*. Next time we play Forgetful Phonics, I'll try leaving out the end sound instead of the beginning, and we'll see what good guessers you are!

After a few sessions of vocal phonics, the teacher is often hard pressed to keep up with the children. Their intense interest in such sound play can be further stimulated by having them begin to participate individually. Such individual participation can be carried out like this:

Let's do Phonics Up Front today! I'd like two volunteers, please. Thank you. All right, Tommy, you stand on my right and Susan, you on my left. You two are "up front" now to help me sound out a word. I'll whisper a sound in your ear and when I touch you on the shoulder, say your sound loud and clear. Tommy, you're the beginning sound; I'll be the middle, and Susan here will be the last sound of our word. The rest of the class is to listen and then tell us what word the three of us have sounded out. (Teacher whispers *mmmm* in Tommy's ear, and *th* in Susan's. She touches Tommy and he says *mmmmm*. The teacher adds *ou*, and Susan ends with *th*.) Who can guess? That is right, *mouth*. Now may I have two more helpers? (The same kind of routine is followed for presenting the various parts of the body: *llll – – e – – g, fff – – ing – – – ger, nnn – – ooo – – zzzz, th – – u – – m*, etc.)

How would you all like to be in the spotlight? I have my flashlight here, and I'm going to give you a chance to play In the Spotlight. This half of the room will say *ai* when the spotlight hits them, and the other half will say *t* when the light flashes to them. I'll make the first sound of the word. Let's try it . . . *k – – – ai – – – t*. Is that hard? I'll say it for you, *k – – ai – t*. Yes, kite. Now, see if you can guess this one without any help. I'll say *llll*. Now: *llll – – ai – – t*. Yes, light. You got that one. Let's try one more with those sounds. I'll say *sssss*. Now watch the light for your turn . . . *sssss – – ai – – – – t*. Yes, *sight* was the word. Good for you!

First- and second-graders often become so proficient in vocal phonic games that the teacher must resort to Backward Vocal Phonics to challenge them. This is a test of their ability in this area, since they must be able to retain the sound sequence in their memory and then reverse it. An example of Backward Phonics might be as follows:

Wouldn't our clothes look funny if we put them on backward? Words sound funny when they are said backwards, too. Just as it is fun to put our mother's and father's old clothes on backwards when we play, it's fun to play with words in the same way. Let me "put on" a word backwards for you and see if you can guess what it is . . . *oooooo – – – – shhhhh.* *Shoe* is right. Be sure and make the last sound you hear, the first sound in the word. Here's another one . . . *oooooh – t.* Make the *t* the first sound . . . yes, that's it, *toe!* Those were easy. Let's see if you can do it with three sounds now. *Ssssss – – – – urrrrrrr – – – – – – p.* Now let's see . . . it's *p – – – urrr – – – now you've got it, *purse!* *llllll – – – awwwwwww – k.* Yes, *call.* I'm going to sound out backwards the name of a boy in this room. Let's see if you can point to him . . . *kk – – – arrrr – mmmm.* Good. Several people pointed to Mark.

# VI
# *Improving Fluency*

🖉 WE TEND to think of the fluent tongue as a natively endowed gift. Our culture rewards the facile speaker in many ways, and most of us envy the person who can express his thoughts fluently. While there are exceptions (those who say little while speaking much), the ability to speak smoothly without hemming and hawing seems actually to improve the formulation of thought. Sloppy speakers are often sloppy thinkers. Incoherency always reflects itself in the rhythm of utterance as well as in the expression of ideas. Listening to hesitant, broken speech is not a pleasant experience; it places too heavy a load upon the listener. This speaker-induced strain often causes the listener, during pauses, to find his mind anticipating and following paths of association which must be retraced when the nonfluent speaker finally gets going again.

If we are to help our children realize the full possibilities inherent in the great tool of speech, we must, somewhere during their schooling, place strong emphasis on fluency. Many teachers, in their effort to be patient and understanding, tolerate far more awkwardness of utterance than they should. They will not tolerate a slipshod paper in the child's written composition, but they accept without question speech which is far from adequate. Fluency is not a gift. It, too, is learned. Few teachers have ever praised a child for fluency, and they must do so if he is ever to master this important skill.

## SETTING THE VOCAL PACE

Many people tend to confuse output with fluency though they are far from synonymous. Some of the most fluent speakers talk rather slowly and deliberately. According to Hayworth,[1] the swiftest speakers are the most nonfluent. Words that tumble over themselves in their rush from the mouth seldom flow smoothly. Each of us seems to have an optimal rate at which we can speak smoothly. When we exceed this natural speed, our tongues stumble as much as our fingers do when typing too fast. The nervous, keyed-up child often works his speech mechanism faster than it can operate efficiently and we need not wonder that his keys stick. Certainly one of the goals which teachers could give their children is an understanding of this concept of a natural vocal pace.

Similarly, there is need to fit the pace of the mouth to the pace of the mind. All of us have known the experience of having our mouths outrun our thoughts. The senior author of this text once took a typing course and, using the touch system, was able to write fifty words per minute. However, he found himself absolutely unable to write original material at this rate and had to return to the old hunt-and-peck two-finger method. The fluent speaker has learned to adjust his rate of speech to the rate of his consecutive thinking. When

[1] Donald Hayworth, *Introduction to Public Speaking*. New York: Ronald Press Company, 1941, p. 223.

both are paralleling each other, utterance and listening both become a pleasure.

How can the teacher help her children to set their individual vocal pace? She certainly would not want to subject a child who speaks nervously and rapidly to the ordeal of exhibiting his speech pattern before the group. She can, however, adopt such a speech pattern herself during a playlet. For example:

Today we'll have a pretend play. I'm going to be two people. When I put on this hat with a feather on it, I'll be a mother. And when I put on this beanie, I'll be that mother's little boy. Your job is to listen to HOW the mother and little boy speak, as well as to what they say. Listen to how fast these people talk when they are upset. . . .

(Teacher puts beanie on.) Hey, ma, I'm home. Gee, we had fun today. . . . I played ball with the fellas down at (speech is fluent up to this point) . . .

(Teacher puts on feathered hat.) Young man, what do you mean by coming home an hour late for supper! What do I have to do to make you remember? This is the second time this week that you disobeyed (uses loud, angry voice) . . .

(Teacher with beanie) But, but, but gee, ma, I didn't know it was so late . . . why, all the fellas, all the fellas, they played, played as long as I, I did . . . I didn't mean to be late (more and more breaks in the fluency of his speech as he realizes his mother is still angry) . . .

(Teacher with hat) Whether you meant to be late or not, you are! I've had just about enough of this. Your dinner is ice cold. Just for that, you march yourself right up to bed . . .

(Teacher with beanie) But, but . . . you said I could watch Roy Rogers tonight . . . you, you promised me, aw, please let me stay up. . . . Honest, ma, I'll remember, I'll be sure to remember next time to come home right on time . . . please, mom, let me stay up and wat, watch television (speech is rapid and broken as he pleads) . . .

(Teacher with hat) That will be just enough out of you. . . . All I ever hear is excuses, excuses. . . . *Get upstairs.*

(Teacher with beanie) Aw, for gosh sakes!

Or the teacher might put her own speech patterns before the class like this:

You know, everyone has his own way of talking. It may be high or low, soft or loud, and slow or fast. You boys and girls listen to me many times during each day. I want you to help me now. Would you tell me whether I'm going fast or slow as I pretend to do different things.

First of all, I'm going to pretend I'm at home, and I have some sewing to do. As I do it, I'm going to be talking. Tell me if I'm talking fast or slow. "Hmmm, now let's see . . . if I put the pattern on the material this way, I may have enough to make some pockets for the skirt . . . let's see . . . now . . . if I . . . just shift . . . this piece. . . ."

How did I sound? Was it fast or slow? Pretty slow, wasn't it? And that's because I was thinking and planning and talking all at the same time. Perhaps you haven't noticed, but I'll bet there's lots of times, when you talk just like that under your breath. Perhaps it's about something else, of course—building a birdhouse, playing a game, or spelling a word.

Now let's see if you can guess whether I'm talking fast or slow. Let's pretend we're all going on a trip to the farm on a school bus. It's warm and the windows are open. You are all kind of wiggly and suddenly I say, "Johnny, don't lean out that window!" How would I say that? Yes, I would say it very fast, wouldn't I? I'd say it fast because I'm worried about Johnny falling out—and I'll say it loudly because I want him to be sure to hear me!

This kind of activity might serve as an introduction for other children in the class to participate in play-acting various vocal paces.

I know that Ralph plays baseball, and he listens to the Tiger games. Ralph, would you show us how the announcer sounds when someone hits a homer? We'll pretend that you are the man on the radio who is broadcasting the game. You make us feel how excited everyone is by the way you tell us about the man, as he hits the ball and it sails out of the park.

Mary Anne's mother works at the public library, and she's their Story-Time Lady. Mary Anne, would you show us how your mother tells a story to the very little boys and girls who come to listen to her? I know you've been there many times. Would you tell us the story of "The Three Bears" just the way your mother would?

## STOPPING THE STALLERS

According to several researches, verbal fluency is in part a function of the richness of word associations and the speed of word association. We all have known the faltering which results from our need to search for the right word. Everything stops until it arrives or else we cover up by using stallers of various sorts, "ers" and "ums" and the multitude of grunts, "ahs," and other sounds used as a filibustering device to gain time. In many cases, we stop, then repeat a previous word or phrase to get us going again. A certain amount of such delay tactics is tolerated by our culture without penalty,

Talk! Don't Grunt!

but they are at best excrescences, and far too many of us permit too many of them to occur. They certainly contribute nothing to efficient communication, except to indicate that the speaker is having trouble and begs the listener not to go away.

These stallers can easily become habitual, a part of the speaker's verbal clothing. Some speakers seem to be almost congenitally unable to utter even the simplest statement without a volley or two. Many a child uses an "um" or an "ah" even as he raises his hand, to show that he is intending to speak. He winds up, like a baseball pitcher, to deliver his verbal pitch, but his windup contributes little to his delivery. We must prevent our children from getting into habits of this sort which later they will regret. Anyone who has ever taught or taken a college public speaking class will recognize how difficult the "stallers" are to eliminate, once they have become unconscious. If, by some training in the elementary school, we can prevent these misplaced oral punctuation marks from becoming part of the speaker's learned language, we will have done much to prepare him for the future.

If the child is to replace such misplaced oral punctuation with adequate speech, he must build a supply of words with which to fill those vacuous and vagrant pauses. Then, too, he must recognize the presence of the stallers before they can be eliminated.

I want each of you to choose a talking partner. Would you stand facing that partner? Good. Now everyone on my right will start talking to his partner. I will time you. You'll start talking and keep talking for two minutes about what you did over the week end. Your partner's job is to keep track of how many "stallers" you use. He will clap his hands each time he hears one. When he has clapped three times, you must sit down. Let's see how many of you can remain standing for the whole two minutes. Get set: Go! (When time is up, switch sides, the silent side now doing the talking, while being checked by their talking partners.)

We will have a Tall Tale story-time today. The first person in the first row will start a story—it can be a silly story or a true story or a sad story. As soon as that person uses a staller, he must sit down and the person in the next seat will stand up and continue his version of our Tall Tale. When he uses a staller, down he goes!

Many such speech games will help to bring those snide little stallers out into the open where they can be captured. Once caught, speech stallers should be disposed of and replaced with a more appropriate utterance.

### SPINNING THE SPEECH DRUMS

The stress upon vocabulary building in the elementary school has not been misplaced. We know how important it is to reading and to writing. However, its importance in the fluency of oral utterance has not been noted by many. Yet, in numerous ways the availability of the right word can make a mighty difference in clarity of thinking and fluency of expression.

Just as there is an eye-voice span in oral reading, so, too, there is a similar scanning process preceding utterance. Our minds keep looking ahead of our mouths, scanning our memory drums for the words which will be needed. If there are few words available, and none just right, we are likely to falter, to hesitate and rephrase in a less adequate fashion. Much of this process is automatic and we are not aware of what is going on until we find a gap where there should be a word. It should be the teacher's function to help fill those holes, to eliminate the gaposis.

It might be felt that the type of vocabulary building which we use in reading should be sufficient. However, the disparity between our recognition vocabulary in reading and our usage vocabulary in writing is well known. We never use as large a vocabulary in the latter. In speaking, our vocabularies are even more restricted, sometimes so thoroughly that we are greatly handicapped in expressing our thoughts. As any good teacher knows, it is through discussion that new words are learned most easily. The usual method is to fix the word, once it has come up, by writing it in a meaningful sentence. Very seldom, however, do we use the same procedure for fixing words in our oral vocabularies. Yet those of us who have trouble in remembering the names of people to whom we have been introduced know that the quickest way of remembering those names is to use them several times in our speech. We teachers must not confine ourselves to teaching a recognition vocabulary. We must get the words into meaningful utterance.

Are grown-ups always making you jump to do as they say? Now here's your chance to play a "make me jump" game. I'm going to say a sentence and you've got to say the same thing in a different way but so it means the same thing. If you can find three ways of saying it, then I'll have to jump. Okay? Here's the sentence: "Oooooh, I'm sick to my stomach." (Class gives answers by raising hands and volunteering.) You made me jump that time. Let's see if you can do it again. Here's another sentence: "I'm glad vacation is coming soon." Can you make me jump?

Here is a different approach for increasing the children's vocabulary fund:

I'm going to see how many different animals you can name. I want everyone to stand up first of all. Then, as I count, you say the name of the animal, like this . . . 1. cats, 2. dogs, 3. . . . When you can't think of another animal's name, sit down. Let's see who can stand up the longest. (The teacher varies this activity by choosing other categories on other days.)

When we first learn to talk, we often use shorter and simpler words then when we grow up and go to school. I'm going to give you the baby name for some things, and I'd like you to give me the grown-up name. Choo–chooo . . . yes, train. Now, let's try some more:

ga' ma   (grandmother)
bunny   (rabbit)
da-da   (father)
baby horsie   (pony)
baby cow   (calf)
wa-wa   (water)

(The teacher has the children respond as a group.)

When we took a trip to John's grandfather's farm last week, we learned the names of many pieces of farm machinery and the names of various places on the farm. We'll play an echo game today! I'll start to say something about the farm, then you say it and fill in the ending. For instance, when I say, "Every morning the cows go out to . . . ," you repeat that and then add the name of the field to which they go. . . . "Every morning the cows go out to *pasture*." Now, let's have you finish these sentences for me:

We played in the hay in the _____ (haymow).
The animals drink water from a _____ (trough).
We saw a man drive a _____ (tractor).
All the chickens sleep in the _____ (henhouse).
The machine that was in the yard was a _____ (cultivator).

## TURNING ON THE VERBAL FAUCET

Since verbal fluency depends not only upon the number of words available but also upon the speed of association, we should help our children get some basic training in this area. Marked individual differences occur in the speed of association, with intelligence being an important factor, but not the only one. We have found that it is possible to gain much skill in speed of association through training. This should not be surprising if we recall that in psychoanalysis, free association at first comes very slowly and with difficulty, but after enough experience, it increases markedly both in speed and in quantity. There are many common blocks to the free output of word associations. Often they are of emotional origin, but sometimes they are due to restrictions in the type of set used. Some children seem to confine themselves to antonyms, to opposites, and find it hard to break free from this pattern. Others use synonyms in the same way. Gradually they can be helped to get more flexibility, to use categories, subordinates, descriptive modifiers, and many others of the infinite possibilities available. Training in controlled association in which the teacher describes the type of response desired (trees: Christmas, maple, elm, etc.) brings rapid returns and much more than one would expect in terms of fluency. Moreover, the children learn much from each other. They enjoy word play of all types, and this form seems to be peculiarly fascinating.

There are times, during our geography or arithmetic classes, when you all try to give me an answer at the same time. During those classes, I often ask you all to be quiet and have just one person at a time give me an answer. However, during speech class today, I want you all to talk at once! I want to see who can talk the longest without saying anything twice! When you can't think of anything more to say, stop and sit down.

I'm going to raise my arms as I say a word, and lower them as I say the opposite. All of you must do the same. Hot (arms up), cold (arms down). Good. Now, I'll just say the first word, and you must give me the second. Short . . .

We're going to play a game today called "Fish and Fowl." When I say "fish," you must give me the name of a kind of fish before my ruler hits the table. When I say "fowl," you must give me the name of a kind of bird. Let's see how many minutes we can go before we're unable to think of another kind. All right . . . "fish". . . yes, Johnny—trout. "Fowl". . . robin, yes. Now again . . . "fish". . .

Speech of association must be taught in such a way that no child becomes pressured beyond his capacity for enjoyment. It is wise to begin at rates far below their basal associative speed and gradually increase them to the point just below the point of faltering and frustration. Then, by returning to the basal speed and repeating the process, it will be found that the child can go farther the second time before he hits his threshold of faltering. For example, if the teacher asks the children as a group to finish her sentence in a whisper before she rings a bell, the time intervals can be controlled appropriately. The use of a metronome set to tick very slowly to time the children's utterance of color names will serve as another example. It must be obvious that many of these activities can be viewed as basic training in thinking. Perhaps one reason it is so painful for so many of us to think is that we have had so little training in these vital skills. At any rate, we do know that such training will improve the fluency of speech and should be given to every child.

I'm going to talk backwards and tell you what to do. "Up stand; nose scratch; foot right, lift; nose on finger put."

While George gets a volleyball from the cloakroom, I'm going to explain a new game we'll play today. I want you all to be ready to catch the ball. I'll toss it to a different person each time, and as soon as you catch it, you must give me a number. The first person I toss it to will say "one"; then he'll toss it to someone else, who must say "two" the minute he catches it; the next person will say "three" and so on. We'll start out throwing the ball to each other rather slowly and then we'll start speeding up until someone can't think of the number the moment he catches it. I wonder how high we'll be able to go this time.

Here's a spool of thread. I'm going to roll it down the length of the library table. As soon as it starts rolling, I want all of you to start naming the other people in the room: "Mary Jones, Pat Johnson, Bill Ford," and so on. Say as many as you can before the spool of thread falls off the other side of the table.

## THE STEADY STREAM

Another phase of this training involves experiences in the "feel of fluency." By this phrase we refer to the sensations of free verbal flow. Children know it well and prize it, as their love of rhyming attests. There is almost sensuous pleasure in

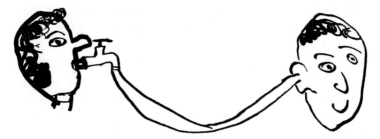

Turn on the Faucet and Let the Speech Flow.

the feedback or echo of words flowing smoothly from the mind via the mouth. Many children experience it vicariously by listening to adults reading to them, but few get enough through self-hearing. The teacher should give them this experience directly. Often echo speech, memorization, choral reading, or unison speech can serve to focus children's attention on this important facet of fluency, but we must be sure that they also recognize it when it occurs in their own spontaneous utterance. The teacher, by her praise, can make this feel of fluency a true goal.

Winston Churchill once said that the feel of a well-ordered phrase was the core of all successful speaking. How often do we find speakers with no sense of phrasing, who use only the need for physiological air as the signal for the momentary pause. The spoken English language is a noble thing when spoken well, but improper phrasing can ruin it. We teachers spend much time with the commas and periods of our chil dren's written compositions but practically none with the pauses which are their oral equivalents.

Not just phrases, but sentences, too, are botched by far too many speakers. Some children often seem to be helplessly trying to stop when reciting but they do not know how to do so because they are plagued by the conjunction "and." One sentence runs into another, and that into a third, all linked by that perpetual conjunction. One of the basic features of the speech of a fluent person is that he ends a sentence cleanly before he begins its successor. How often do we hear our children starting their recitations strongly and bravely, only to trail off into an embarrassed and weak nothingness of a conclusion! We must, then, create a "feel" for a good sentence in speech as well as in writing, helping our children sense a need for driving through to the period and then stopping. Can this be taught? He who feels it cannot has little appreciation of the tremendous powers of imitation children possess. It need not be taught through penalty or rejection, so that threat interferes with fluency, but through the providing of models, both good and poor, which they can learn to discriminate. Such discrimination will help them to discipline the structure of their own speech.

Rhythm plays an important part in the sensation of free verbal flow. Nursery rhymes swing along to a short—at times staccato—beat. They endure regardless of their ancient aroma and the efforts of some educators to dismiss them from the realm of childhood's immortal "literature." The rhythm of the rhymes attracts the children long before they know why Mary is contrary or Jack is nimble. At a very young age they serve as a conveyer of fluency. Whatever transmits the feel of fluency through rhythm should be fostered. Verbal flow may be reinforced by the teacher through various choral reading and unison speaking activities. Echo speech, as its name implies, can serve as a strong fluency reinforcing agent. The teacher sets the standard of fluency, with the children imitating this standard in every detail as her echo.

I want you to be my echoes. You must say exactly what I say in exactly the same way. I'll raise my hand as I finish each sentence and then you all echo it together. "I'm lost. . . . This is a strange place. . . . Where do I turn? . . . Which way is home? . . . Where's my mother? . . . Oh, there she is! . . . Mother. . . . Mother. . . . I'm so glad to see you. . . . I'm not lost any more!"

Here's a picture of children playing at a beach. I'm going to tell you about the things that are happening in the picture, but I'm only going to start the sentence; you must finish it. This little boy is . . . (Children chime in with "throwing a ball.") These little girls are building . . . The seagulls are flying above . . . The waves are . . . The children in the water are . . . (The teacher varies this activity by having many kinds of action pictures.)

Here's another "finish it for me" game. Last night I told a story to my little girl, and while I was telling it, I made a recording of it. I have the tape recorder here and I'm going to play back the story for you. Listen hard and when I turn down the volume so that you can't hear the end of the sentence, I'd like to have all of you finish the sentence for me.

This is a film strip on farm animals. I'm going to show it to you and describe each picture. When I'm done, I'll turn the strip back to the beginning and I want all of you to describe the pictures to me in unison. I'll make the film strip go very slowly at first so that you will have enough time.

## BETTER BUILT BARRIERS

Finally, we can help our children master fluent speech by helping them build barriers against the influences which destroy fluency. Some children have so low a threshold of resistance that they falter the moment the teacher glances in some other direction. Surely we can toughen them in some degree. Some of the most common fluency disrupters are these: interruptions, hurry, competition for the listener's ear, the loss of a listener, an unfavorable reaction on the part of the listener, and noise.

How can we build these barriers? Again we use the principle of desensitization. Telling the children what we are going to use as a fluency disrupter, we start them out saying something which they know well and can say fluently. Then we introduce the disrupting influence (e.g., the noise) and put

There's a Need to Build Barriers so We Can Be Fluent.

them on their mettle to resist it. By gradually increasing the disrupting influence, the heckling, or whatever we are using, and making sure that they always win but are pushed pretty close to the limit, we will see them gain greatly in barrier building. It is surprising to note the generalization and transfer of these experiences to other situations and to other disturbing influences never used in the actual training. What the child learns evidently is how to be fluent under stress.

I want each of you to pretend to be talking to a friend on the telephone. You're to tell your friend what you did at school today. While you're all talking, I'm going to walk around and try to interrupt each of you. Now, when I come around to your seat, you keep right on talking no matter what I say. Let's see how many of you will be able to keep on talking to your friend.

I'm going to divide the room in half. I want the right-hand side of the room to recite the numbers I've written on the board. I want the left-hand side of the room to recite the days of the week. Let's see which side can talk the loudest and longest!

I want you to start counting—1, 2, 3, and so on. You're to count in rhythm with me, however; I'm going to start tapping very slowly and then speed up. Let's see how long you can all count and keep up with my tapping.

Let's talk about a birthday party—the kind of birthday party you'd like to have. I'm going to listen and look at you for a while, and then I'm going to be very busy checking the materials on my desk. I want you to keep on talking, even though I'm not listening. Be sure to keep on talking as long as you can. (Teacher climaxes it by walking out the door, and then reappearing a moment or two later.) Did anyone keep on talking about the birthday party even though I walked out of the room?

# VII
## Thinking Aloud

✎ ONE OF the most ancient and yet most important goals of education is that of training the child to think more efficiently. Socratic questioning, the verbal disciplines of the Hindu mystics, the interminable oral recitation of memorized material by the Chinese, the metaphysical debates by the scholars of the Middle Ages, and the present emphasis upon discussion and group interaction all make clear the close connection between thinking and speaking. The essence of thought is that it enables us to manipulate symbols instead of physical things. The physicist uses mathematical symbols for his thinking; most of us use words.

### SPOKEN SYMBOLS

Is it possible to improve our children's ability to think? The constancy of the I.Q. and the failure to show much transfer of training from such mental disciplines as algebra, Latin, or mental arithmetic to other related activities may seem to deny such a possibility. However, we might remember that an I.Q. may represent only the person's facility in handling symbols and that no subtest of the Binet, for example, correlates more highly with the total score than does that which measures vocabulary. We could hardly expect

III

that training in manipulating the visual symbols of algebra would show a marked transfer to such a skill as memorizing verbal symbols or that learning Latin conjugations would help us in geometry. But we must remember that in learning or problem solving of any kind some form of language process is involved. As Vinacre says, "All thinking involves the previous experience of the individual and is therefore basically the transfer of that experience to the present situation."[1] This transfer is primarily verbal though not necessarily vocal. Wesman found that there was no transfer to intelligence scores from any of several school achievement experiences and states that there was a need for direct training in mental processes rather than dependence on transfer from school subjects.[2] Morris declares: "Training in the flexible use of symbols means gaining the ability to enter into fruitful interaction with persons whose symbols differ from one's own."[3] In John Dewey's classical analysis of thinking (1. perplexity, doubt, confusion; 2. analyzing the problem and setting up possible solutions; 3. organizing the data to clarify the problem; 4. selecting tentative hypotheses; and 5. testing and verifying them) the importance of implicit speech is apparent.

Language appears to be very close to the base of truly symbolic processes. Rugg and Shumaker say: "Free the legs, the arms, the larynx of a child and you have taken the first

[1] W. Edgar Vinacre, *The Psychology of Thinking*. New York: McGraw-Hill Book Company, 1952, p. 60.

[2] Alexander Wesman, "A Study of Transfer of Training from High School Subjects to Intelligence," *Teacher's College Record*, Vol. 46, 1945, p. 393.

[3] Charles Morris, *Signs, Language and Behavior*. New York: Prentice-Hall, Inc., 1946, p. 246.

step toward freeing his mind and spirit."[4] Guthrie and Powers point out that children's activity in the classroom is largely limited to talk, so classroom teaching is going to be confined largely to speech habits. "Probably the activities of most interest in education center about speech and the establishment of new verbal habits. . . . It is the teacher's job to incite and guide inner speech and the spoken word."[5]

These quotations are sufficient to indicate that psychologists and educators alike appreciate the importance of spoken language in the early school years. Speech therapists have long known that children with delayed speech show phenomenal gains in I.Q. and school achievement once they acquire some facility in talking. Certainly, some basic training in oral communication skills should benefit the normal child.

### LANGUAGE PROCESS

That few of us who are adults have reached a high level of skill in expressing our thoughts orally should be evident to any perceptive person. Surely those of us who listen to the recitations of college students, who wonder at the faltering and foggy oral meanderings of most contributors to parent-teacher meetings, who scrutinize the confused arguments and awkward reasoning of our friends must recognize a need for more experience and training in expressing our thoughts aloud. But how can this be acquired?

The senior author of this book gathered 5000 samples of the speech of elementary children spoken during play in or-

[4] H. Rugg and A. Shumaker, *The Child Centered School*. Chicago: World Book Company, 1928, p. 55.

[5] Edwin Guthrie and Francis F. Powers, *Educational Psychology*. New York: Ronald Press Company, 1950, p. 141.

der to study the types of communicative utterance being used. He was surprised to find that 85 percent of the utterance of kindergarten and first-grade children had no element of communication in it; they were merely talking to themselves. The percentage of this self-talk decreased markedly in the second and higher grades, however. This trait has been noted by other investigators. Piaget describes it in this fashion: the child "talks either for himself or for the pleasure of associating anyone who happens to be there with the activity of the moment. . . . He feels no desire to influence his hearer or tell him anything. . . . These ego-centric remarks, as opposed to questions, orders, or adapted information, consisted for the most part of soliloquies and of a kind of pseudo-conversation or collective monologues in the course of which children speak to themselves and pay no attention to each other. . . . The chief function of this ego-centric language is therefore to serve as an accompaniment to the thought and action of the individual."[6]

Watson says it this way:

The child talks incessantly when alone. . . . Aloud he voices his wishes, his hopes, his fears, his annoyances, his dissatisfactions with his nurse or his father. Soon society in the form of nurse or parents steps in. "Don't talk aloud. . . . Daddy and mother are not always talking to themselves." Soon the overt speech dies down to a whispered speech and a good lip reader can still read what the child thinks of the world and himself. Some individuals never even make this concession to society. When alone they talk to themselves. A still larger number never go beyond the whispering stage when alone. Watch people reading on the street car; peep through the keyhole sometimes when individuals not too highly socialized are just sitting and thinking.

[6] Jean Piaget, *The Language and Thought of the Child*. New York: Harcourt, Brace and Company, 1926, p. 9.

But the great majority of people pass on to the third stage under the influence of social pressure constantly exerted. "Quit whispering to yourself" and "Can't you even read without moving your lips?" and the like are constant mandates.[7]

## SELF-TALK

In examining our collected samples of self-talk, we found that the great majority were comments on what the child was *perceiving, doing,* or *feeling.* He was accompanying these three phases of his consciousness by a running commentary, giving himself a verbal play-by-play account of what was going on. Often it had some similarity to a radio announcer's description of a prize fight or horse race. What was the child doing in his self-talk? What function does it have?

Our conclusion was that self-talk has a real utility. It serves as the vehicle for teaching the child to think. Perhaps the child knows what all the educators have forgotten—that it is possible to learn to think, and that the initial step in acquiring this facility is through self-talk. By associating verbal symbols with all the features of his experience he gains the ability to use that experience in the future. He can remember it more easily; he can fit it into new patterns. Even as the physicist turns his data into numerical symbols and equations so that he can handle them more easily and understand the basic nature of the physical world, so also does the child translate his perception, action, and emotion into verbal symbols, and for the same reason.

It is tragic that we adults find thinking so difficult. We find it hard to size up a situation realistically and intelligently. We find it far from easy to plan our actions in terms

[7] John B. Watson, *Behaviorism*. New York: People's Institute Publishing Company, 1925, p. 193.

of our future goals or our present abilities as we know them from the past. Edison once said that he could never understand why thinking was so painful for most people. Our answer is that we have been prevented by our schools and our paranoid culture from exploiting our self-talk. Edison was stone deaf and talked to himself constantly.

Little children know instinctively that thought must be fluent to be effective. They know that autistic speech is the one basic invention which gives them mastery of the future. It is the peculiarly human gift. Having just mastered the use of this magical tool, small children are busy using it. They express what they see; they say what they do; they tell what they feel. They are trying hard to learn how to talk to themselves fluently.

### SPEECH A BASIC SKILL

Few of us appreciate the importance of speech in learning. We tend to consider reading the basic skill. But what happens when we understand the words on the printed page? We have been talking to ourselves. In this silent self-talking only the poorest students echo the words they are reading and then they do not comprehend. Many a student complains, "This stuff is so dry that I read it over and over again and it's just so many words." What he means is that he is unable to translate the printed letters into the language of self-talking. You have had the same experience when reading while tired.

Some of us talk aloud to ourselves when alone. Often, when engaged in a task like upholstering a chair, you will find yourself saying, "No, I can't do it that way. I'll just . . . have to . . . put the seam . . . over there. . . . Sure, I've got to reverse it. That's it!" Talking to yourself aloud is frowned upon by our culture. If we do it in the wrong places we end up on the psychiatrist's couch, and then he encourages us to think aloud.

Actually, self-talking goes on throughout our whole lives. It is vitally necessary to all thought. Many psychologists feel that it *is* thought. The stream of consciousness is a verbal stream. We solve problems by first stating the problem, by asking questions of ourselves. Then we try out one possible solution after another, thinking it out in words if we can, or silently commenting on our various attempts as we carry them out. The more fluent one's self-talking, the better he can think.

But you say, "We can't go through our lives talking to ourselves. People would think we were insane." Adults do not read aloud either, but most of them began by doing oral reading. Gradually, as they became fluent in their oral reading, silent reading appeared. Soon they found themselves reading whole phrases and even sentences. Why can't something of the same process be duplicated in speech? Actually, this is exactly what happens. The trouble is, however, that our school systems do not train us in self-talking. We never get a chance to do it fluently and openly. Before we can self-talk easily aloud, the clamps are put on. We get shushed. Another iron curtain comes down.

## SELF-TALK IN THE SCHOOLROOM

Unless we look at our schoolrooms with new eyes, we never realize how strong is the taboo against self-talking. Even in the most progressive of modern schools it gets little encouragement. A permissive atmosphere is not enough. The self-direction of activities is neither sufficient nor entirely wise. Our schools should train children to perceive with insight, to act intelligently, and to handle their emotions. This means helping them to verbalize what is going on. Our schools have been criticized because they have failed to teach children to think. Good teachers try to do just that, and many of them succeed. But when they do, it is because their children have been indirectly encouraged to do just what we have been stressing here. They have been helping a child to talk to himself, to comment on his perceptions, actions, and feelings as they occur. Socrates was a wonderful teacher, and the Socratic method is just one of many devices to help a person talk to himself.

It might well be objected that a schoolroom in which every student thought out loud would be pandemonium indeed. We are not, of course, suggesting this. What we are suggesting is that during the speech improvement period children find the permissiveness and encouragement needed to facilitate the self-talk which can make the inner speech more fluent. This is the time for self-talk, for the running commentary on things perceived, actions occurring, and feelings experienced. This is the time for priming the pump, so that ideas may be felt to flow smoothly instead of painfully by fits and starts. Some time during the busy school day should certainly be reserved for this most important function.

### THE SELF-TALK SEQUENCE

There are various levels of self-talk: the primitive level of the appropriate gesture seen in the emphatic pushing of one's neighbor at a football team, the gasp of the child watching a film of cowboys and villains. Some of us get too rigid in our postural activities too soon and we lose much appreciation when exposed to vicarious experiences so vital to education. In our speech improvement time, we can help children retain the emphatic imitative freshness with which they came to us. The next level of self-talk is the level of free association, of the stream of consciousness. This is essentially a fluent process, as daydreaming demonstrates. Only when it is censored or when emotionally loaded memories emerge does it begin to falter. It is the stuff out of which creative thinking comes. Surely we can give our children some experience in this vital area. Next we reach the level of controlled thinking, of determined organization of ideas, of fitting words to fulfill a preconceived set or nascent attitude. This is where most of us run into trouble. Here is where we become nonfluent in our thinking. But we have found that, when the pump is primed by preceding experiences in gestural self-talk and free association, propositional thinking becomes much more fluent, much more highly organized and efficient.

Therefore the part of our speech improvement period which we devote to this phase usually follows the sequence described. First we get the postural responses of the children flowing freely in response to stimulation. Then we give them some experience in verbalized stream-of-consciousness utterance in the presence of that stimulation. Next we get them to do the running commentary on what is being perceived, carried out, or felt. Finally, we create a problem situation to which the children react by working out the solution through the oral expression of their thinking. Training of this sort is basic to the skill of being able "to think on your feet," to express your thoughts coherently. It gives the child freedom truly to think aloud without constantly being subjected to social pressure or penalty as he often is in ordinary recitation. The whole experience is a very pleasant one for the children, and thinking does not become invested with pain as is so often the case in our schools.

Here are some examples of how "thinking aloud" training can be presented:

Today we're going to do some thinking out loud about something I know you all find fascinating—cowboys and cattle rustlers. The first thing to do is saddle up your horses and climb on them. Clear off your desks, and we'll use the arm of the desk as the saddle. Everyone, up! Now we're riding along a dusty trail— and suddenly we meet Roy Rogers and Dale Evans. (Teacher brings out appropriate hand puppets.)

All the girls can pretend that they're Dale Evans and all the boys, Roy Rogers. Now, I want you to make up a story about Dale and Roy and a gang of cattle rustlers. You tell me what you'd do, and I'll have my puppets act it out as you make up the story. (Teacher manipulates puppets as children make up the story. Then she stops them at an interesting point in the story.)

Now I'm going to have the puppets act out what happens next. I want you to tell me exactly what Dale and Roy are doing and thinking, by the motions these puppets make. If you're guessing correctly, Dale and Roy will nod to show you that you're on the right track. (Teacher acts out sequence with puppets right up to a climax.)

That's right. Dale and Roy are trapped in a cabin, and the cattle rustlers have convinced some Indians that they must burn down the cabin because Dale and Roy will bring evil spirits to their tribes. The Indians are preparing flaming arrows to shoot at the cabin. I want all of you to think hard and let's see if we can figure out more than just one way of helping Dale and Roy get themselves out of this! There must be several ways that Dale and Roy can save themselves. What do you think? (Teacher helps children to think through an answer orally, reminding them when necessary of the various facets of the problem.)

With the emphasis on cowboy films during the hours devoted to television by the current crop of small fry, such problems and actions as are posed above will be elementary.

You've played lots of different games on the playground, and you have watched lots of other kinds of games on television. I want to see how good you are at "game guessing." I'm going to act out the way to play a certain game. I want you to repeat my actions, and then, anyone who thinks he can guess the name of the game, raise your hand and tell us. (Teacher hits baseball, "makes" a basket, swings a golf club, throws a football, etc.)

The gym teacher told me the other day that the game you all liked to play best was kick-ball. We're going to play a game right now; at least, we're going to pretend we have a ball and do all the things we do when we play the game. Only this time we're going to say out loud what we're thinking as we play the game. Lots of times you think things like, "Gee, if I could just kick the ball over there, no one could get it," or "I wish they'd kick it to me—I haven't even had a chance at it yet." So let's have a talking game this time. We'll talk all the time we're playing, either about what we're doing or want to do or are feeling.

Joan, you come up and stand on this side for your team, and Carl, you stand on the other side. You two are going to be the announcers for each side. I want you to describe what is going on among your team members—everything they do as they play the game.

That was a good game. Carl's side won by five points. But for the moment, let's imagine that Carl's and Joan's teams both had the same number of points just before the end of the game. Someone on Joan's team made a point—at least, Joan's team is sure he made that point; Carl's side is just as sure that he didn't. How would you find out which side was right?

Children often verbalize their feelings during games in which they actively participate since they empathize so greatly with the other players. The physical activity itself seems to serve as a stimulus for speech.

There is often a great deal of autistic thinking and speaking among early elementary children, although parents and teachers do their best to force "reality" upon them. Instead of suppressing such imagery constantly, an outlet can be provided for its expression during the speech improvement period.

There are times when we all want to be the boss; when we do only what we want to do; when we can make everyone else in the whole world do exactly as we say; when we don't have to mind anyone, not even our fathers and mothers. Let's suppose you are all kings and queens, sitting on your thrones. You can make anyone do just as you please. Show me how you'd sit on your thrones!

Now I want you to whisper out loud just what you'd make everyone do. What would be the very first thing you'd make your mother and father do? Your sister or brother? What would you make me do? Remember that you can have anything you'd like. Say out loud everything that you'd like to have and like to do.

Joan said she would help me today. She's put on a crown, and she'll be a queen. Joan and I are going to act out a story. The rest of you are to tell what we're doing and feeling from our actions and the way we look.

You've seen Joan and me act out a story of a queen who did just as she pleased and never thought about anybody but herself. Now I want you to figure out something. Do you think the queen was a happy person? Do you think she would be happier if she'd do things differently? What would you do if you were that queen?

Favorite experiences of childhood make an excellent subject for "thinking out loud." The children's imagination is stirred when, for example, a "circus" or "Christmas" is used as a basis for a speech improvement period.

Lots of you went to the circus when it came to town this spring. Do you remember what it was like? The animals, and the clowns and the popcorn and spun sugar? And how it was hard to watch everything in all three rings at the same time? You had to lean forward and look up to watch all those people performing in the air on the trapeze. Pretend that you are sitting in the bleachers under a circus tent.

I have some pictures here about what happens under the "Big Top." Each picture shows something that happens in the circus. As I show each one, I want you to tell me what you think you would do if you were the person in the picture. Here . . . here's a girl riding bareback on a white horse. What would you be doing if you were this girl and traveled with the circus? Would you be afraid of horses? Would it be easy to stand on the horse's back? . . . And here's a clown—he's standing on his head. If you were that clown, how would you act? . . .

Here's Bobo the clown. He is a marionette and can do all sorts of things. I'll make him perform and you describe everything that he does.

A long time ago, in a city called Boston, there was a big circus fire and lots of boys and girls, and grown-ups, too, were killed. What would you do if you were at a circus, sitting high up on the bleachers, and a fire started?

The above serves merely as an indication of some of the activities that might be used as a basis for a "thinking aloud" sequence. It is the teacher who supplies most of the stimulation and impetus toward speech and who helps the children carry through the series of self-talk activities.

The children, after a sufficient number of self-talk activities, need a more diversified and larger number of experiences in controlled thinking and speaking. When children recite,

Thinking on Your Feet.

the teacher often feels that they do not know how to organize their ideas or to present the material even though they know it well. The ability to "think on one's feet," to combine mind and tongue so that fluent thinking and speech are the result, can be increased through practice. It is, however, an individual process and each child must be given the opportunity to practice fluent and forceful speech with but little time for forethought. Opportunities to think on one's feet might be handled thus:

When we visited the fire station last week, Mr. Young told us a lot about the fire engines, the way they put out fires, the manner in which they received word that there was a fire, and so on. When we came back from the station, we talked about all the things we had learned. Now that several days have gone by, I'd like to know how much we all remember about the trip. I'd like to have Joyce start. Would you come up to the front of the room and tell us what we did when we first got to the station? I've set this clock and the alarm will go off in two minutes. . . . Joyce must talk to us for that length of time. When the alarm goes off, Joyce will point to someone else to take her place and tell us something different about the fire station. Two minutes later, another one of you will be chosen by the person standing in the front of the room. Each person must tell the class something different about the trip.

Another technique is to present the children with a challenge; introduce something which they have not previously studied, and then have them attempt to explain the unknown. For example, one teacher we know did this:

Here's a film strip about wild animals who live in the woods. We haven't learned anything about these particular animals in class, but I'd like to see how much you can guess from what you see in the pictures. I'll ask a different person to tell us about each picture. As soon as I flip to the next picture and call your name, come up and stand by the screen so that you can point to anything in the picture that needs explaining. If you are unable to get enough clues from the picture to tell us about it, make up a story about the animal in the picture, and the way he lives in the woods.

Organizing the information to be presented often constitutes a problem to any speaker, whether child or adult. Knowing what to say and how to say it cannot be learned from one or two speech periods. However, the teacher can help her children learn to organize their material in a logical sequence. Topics which lend themselves to orderly development are those which include a series of actions or processes. Using a hobby display in a second-grade room as the focal point, the teacher suggested that the children each do something like this:

Dave made the model airplane you see on the end of the table. Dave, I'd like to have you get your plane and tell the rest of us just how you built it. Start at the beginning and show us the steps you had to go through before it was all finished.

Mary, you told me you were taking swimming lessons. Would you tell us the things you've learned about breathing and how to use your arms and legs in swimming? Did you learn anything about water safety?

Bob's hobby is music. He's brought his violin today. You know, a violin has to be tuned before you can start playing it. Bob's going to tell us about the things he must do before he can play a piece.

A somewhat more imaginative and revealing activity was attempted by a first-grade teacher when she introduced this:

Today we'll play a game called "If I Were _____" I know all of you have thought about what you'd like to be when you grow up: a nurse, or a fireman, or a dancer, or a cowboy, or something else. Now close your eyes and picture yourself all grown up and being the person you'd like to be. When you feel a tap on your shoulder, stand up and start telling us about your job: "If I were a nurse, I'd take care of sick people and I'd help to make them feel better. I'd be in a big hospital with shiny halls and ambulances!"

We have found that the children at first attempt things like this in a halting but hilarious manner. After just two or three of such sessions involving "thinking aloud," their speech and their thoughts seem to flow much more easily and smoothly, and they look forward eagerly to this kind of activity.

# VIII
## *The Improvement of Voice*

❧ ONE OF the least appreciated of all personal assets is the human voice. We seldom hear our own voices and that is often a good thing; they are so unpleasant that when we hear them for the first time via a playback of recordings we are shocked indeed.

### VANISHING VOICES

We hear only our thoughts as they emerge from our mouths. We are much more interested in what we say than in how we say it. But we should remember that our listeners will make their judgments of us not alone upon the content of our utterance but also upon the way we sound. From earliest infancy we are trained to listen to the tones of the human voice. They tell us if our mothers are angry or tired or loving or impatient. Later on, after we have discovered that words do not always mean what they say and that we must listen also to the inflections which tell us whether or not we can trust the speaker, we find this listening to tones of even greater importance. It is more difficult, we soon learn, for a speaker to deceive us in the way he handles his voice than it is by means of his words. And so, in many instances, the voice itself plays a large part in determining the impression we make upon others, much more than we realize. It is one of the basic attributes of personality.

But voices are learned. When parents whine, children become querulous and nasal. The loud-mouthed father begets either a loud-mouthed child through identification and imitation or a cowed, timorous weak-voiced offspring by conquest or rebellion. Parents often are confounded by hearing their own words and voices issuing from the mouths of babes.

Children also get their voices from each other, often imitating the group leader. Sometimes, identification with a teacher, a movie star, a TV cowboy, a tough gangster, or some other model will produce surprising changes in a pre-adolescent's voice.

At times, voices are learned as a response to the types of demands placed upon the speaker. The shrill strained shrieking of the playground, the hoarse shouts of the athletic field take their toll. The child who does most of his speaking in the classroom beset by the fear that his answers will be wrong will be unlikely to develop a voice of adequate carrying power. The child who at home meets frequent rejection, teasing, or penalty for his verbal volunteering will not tend to show normal inflections or intensity variations. While we cannot control many of these forces bearing upon the child, we may at least show him that there are other voices which he could use in different situations.

## CHANGING VOICES

Few of us ever realize the possibilities of vocal variation permitted us. Instead we fall into habits of voice production, many of them unpleasant and inefficient. Any teacher will testify that many of her children cannot make themselves

Use Your Voice Box.

heard even within the schoolroom. Breathy, hoarse, harsh, nasal, muffled, throaty, falsetto, monotonous, and weak voices are to be heard in any group. Most of their possessors need not speak this way but they have never known until too late that they own many voices, and among them some very good but unused ones. Somewhere in our schooling we should offer some opportunity for children to realize their vocal possibilities.

### VOICE ACTIVITIES

The speech improvement activities dealing with voice betterment involve training in the following areas: hearing one's own voice in terms of pitch, loudness, and quality; hearing the voices of others, comparing and contrasting them with one's own; exploring all the different types of vocal variations possible; negative practice of the less acceptable forms; practice in flexibility of pitch control and inflection; learning to project the voice without increasing the pitch; and working to get a tonal quality pleasant to the listener's ear.

### HEARING ONESELF

While many adults possess little knowledge of their own voices, children seem to have even less ability to hear themselves. Most parents, in fact, would swear that their children are impervious to noise and are constitutionally incapable of lowering their voices below a bellow while playing. Screams, squeaks, squeals, and squawks are standard sounds on the playground, as any adult within palpitating eardrum distance will attest. The only possible conclusion is that the children fail to hear themselves not only as to volume but as to pitch and quality as well.

How can we help them hear themselves? A tape or wire recorder may be an obvious choice if one is available. It presents a flexible method for allowing children to hear themselves as they really sound. Elementary teachers of our acquaintance have devised several methods for using the recorder. First, they successfully secreted the recorder and made a tape while the children were engaged in a free discussion period, such as sharing time or project work. They then played back the tape during a speech improvement period, asking the children to identify their own voices. Other self-speech samples can be recorded during more formal work. Reading groups, recitation periods, and student plays provide opportunities for recording children's voices during actual speech performances. Children are greatly intrigued when the tape is replayed and they must jump up at the sound of their

It's Fun to Record Your Voice.

own voices. If a recorder is not available, other devices to stimulate self-listening must be used.

Today many of you will have a chance to be a pirate. This big cardboard box will be your cave, where you are able to hide and to speak freely. Outside the cave you must whisper, so that you will not be caught by the king's men, but inside the cave you can talk out loud. You'll remember that yesterday we started the story about a little boy who found himself aboard a pirate ship. Today I want you each to take turns—when you enter the cave you are Long John Silver talking to the little boy. You are to make up an end to the story he was telling the boy about his adventures. Listen to how your voice sounds as you talk in the cave!

Clap your hands tightly over your ears as you speak. How does your voice sound? Is it louder or softer? Start counting and when you reach "five," take your hands away from your ears for a few moments and put them back when you reach "ten." Did you notice any difference?

We're going to call the corner of the room by my desk the "Talking Corner," where you can stand and listen to your voice bounce back from both walls. Each of you will pretend to be three animals—first a mouse with a high squeaky voice, next a dog with a medium-sized voice, and third a big brown bear with a deep, gruff voice. Try and make your three voices sound as different as possible. When you've finished, we'd like to know which animal's voice you liked the best.

Here are some paper bags to put over your heads. After you've put them on, say your name to yourself. First try saying it loudly, and then softer and softer. Then try saying it in a high voice, and then make your voice get lower and lower. Listen very carefully. Decide how loud or soft you like to hear it; then decide how high or low. Take off your bag and say your name the way you like it best.

## COMPARING VOICES

While children are delicately attuned to every inflection and shade of meaning in their parents' or teachers' voices, there is little or no self-appraisal of their own voice qualities, and they tend to regard their compatriots' voices with the same bland liberalism. As in so many things, discrimination is based on comparison. Children must be able to discriminate between various voices, including their own, before they can sit in self-judgment and develop standards by which they can improve their voices.

Though you may never have stopped to think about it, you can often guess how old someone is by the way his voice sounds.

Over the week end I made a recording of some people who came to visit me. Today I'd like to have you guess how old they are. I'll give you this much of a hint: there was a baby, a child just about your age, a daddy, and a grandmother. I'll stop the recorder after you hear each of the voices. Tell me how old you think the person with that voice is.

I've paired off the children in the room. If you will look on the board, you will see your name with another name beside it. Before anyone talks at all, we're going to guess which voice is louder and which voice is higher. After we've guessed all the pairs and I've written down our guesses, each couple will get up and tell us the names of their favorite cowboys. We'll be able to see if we were right: just which one speaks more loudly, and which one speaks in a higher tone of voice than the person he happened to be paired with today.

I've got two play telephones that really work, and I've put one in the cloakroom and one here. I'm going to see how good you are at identifying the other children by their voices alone. I'm going to blindfold Susie, and then some of the rest of you will take turns using the other telephone. Susie's job is to identify the other person by the way that person says, "Hello, Susie."

During the next five minutes, I want you each to talk with as many other children as you have time for. Your job is to find the person whose voice sounds the most like yours. You've heard about people who look alike but are not twins—well, you won't find anyone whose voice is exactly like yours, but you will find someone whose voice is more like yours than anyone else's in the room. Let's see how many of you can find a "Sound-Alike" before the five minutes are up.

## VOCAL VARIETY

During their periods of babbling, babies experiment with all kinds of sounds and noises, as a part of learning to talk, often producing sounds which do not exist in the English language. Although this is part of the charm of babyhood, parents begin almost at once to restrict the child's utterances to those which approximate their own speech standards. Most children, conservative and conforming, follow this lead, and by the time they enter school many no longer experiment with the wide range of vocal variations which exist. They may whisper or sing to themselves when alone, but this solitary sound and voice experimentation almost disappears by the time they are six or seven. The flexibility of their voices changes into more stereotyped patterns as the confines and dictates of society draw more closely in upon them. To help them maintain a degree of flexibility and a knowledge of the wide range of voice possibilities, speech improvement periods can be used for voice experimentation.

Yesterday we listed on the blackboard all your favorite television programs. Today we're going to use that list for a television guessing game. We'll take turns imitating the voices of the stars of the television programs, and the rest of the group will guess the name or the program on which the star appears. The better able you are to imitate the voice, the better able we will be to guess the name of the star.

The music teacher left her piano with us today, so that we could use it for an experiment. We're going to see how far up the piano keys you can say "ah," and how far down, without straining. Everyone start at once—but when you feel that you have to try too hard, stop. . . . That's fine. We went up the keys quite a way, but not down very far. Now, all of you turn around so that you can't see the piano. Listen while I strike a key. As soon as you hear it, say your first name at the same tone. We'll try several different tones. Be sure to say your name each time I hit the keys.

Today we're going to visit a zoo. I've arranged some big chairs to form a cage with bars. Everyone will get a chance to be a different animal or bird. When you get in the cage you must show us by your actions and the sounds you make whether you are a lion, a tiger, a bear, an elephant, a monkey, or whatever you may choose to be. The rest of us will guess the kind of bird or beast you are imitating.

If you were a space cadet and visited other planets in the universe, you would find that the people living there might talk differently from the way we do. Ann and Phillip will be our space cadets today, and everyone in the first row will be people living on Mars. They speak an entirely different language and are frightened and worried about these two strangers from the planet Earth. How do you think they would talk and act? Show us by acting it out in the front of the room.

## HOW-TO BY HOW-NOT

Psychologists have found that an excellent method for establishing a correct response is through *deliberate* practice of the incorrect response. By making the response conscious, the entire learning act is emphasized and the differentiation between the correct and incorrect is defined more clearly. Thus, by negative practice of the less acceptable forms of voice variation, the more acceptable forms are more easily recognized and imitated. Some of this ear training is accomplished by having the teacher illustrate some less acceptable voice variations:

Some voices are pretty and some are not. I'm going to give you a sample of four different voices. Tell me if you think they are pretty or not. (Imitates a whiny high-pitched voice; a hoarse "gravel" voice; a nasal voice; and a pleasant voice.) How many did you think you'd like to listen to all day long? Which one did you like the least?

Today we'll use the recorder. I want each of you to be an old mean witch—and to talk in the most unpleasant voice you can manage. Then you'll be the Good Fairy—try to make your voice sound as happy and good as you can. When we play the recording back, let's pick the best Mean Witch and the best Good Fairy.

There are ways of changing your voices without pretending to be someone else. For example, everyone hold his nose and talk through his mouth. . . . Do you hear what a different voice that gives you? Now, snort your words, making them come out your nose. Finally, try talking without letting your tongue move up and down, and see what happens to your speech.

Here's Groucho, my new puppet. Groucho feels badly because no one likes to listen to his voice. Listen to him talk, and then tell what you think is wrong. Can you imitate him? Can you make your voice sound the way his does? Let's all try it. (Groucho says: "I don't like school". . . .) Everyone say that the way Groucho did.

### PITCHING A CURVE

While there is a great deal of unconscious inflection and pitch change in the voices of children, any direct effort to make children control their pitch and inflection results in a stilted form of speech. All of us have encountered children who read with "expression," but it is far from a natural mode of speech. Their voices rise and fall according to punctuation marks rather than the content of the reading material, and they exhibit a stereotyped pitch and inflection as long as they are reading. Our problem is to help them recognize pitch and inflection variations in their own voices, and to use their voices in a natural but flexible manner.

Jimmy and Dale are going to put on a play for us. They're going to act out a story about a boy who gets a new bike and another boy who takes it without asking first. We aren't going to be able to see them because they will be behind the screen, but we'll be able to hear everything they say. All of you have paper and pencil in front of you. . . . We're going to draw lines to represent their voices as we hear them go up and down— a red line for Jimmy and a blue line for Dale. Let's see how many of us can keep up with them.

You all know that it isn't always *what* someone says but the *way* he says it that may be important. Just by listening to the voice instead of the words we can often tell how another person is feeling. There are some words on the blackboard—"Hi," "Good morning," "Good night," and "Be quiet." Let's see how many different ways we can think of to say each of those phrases. We will start with the first row. Each person is to say one of those words and the rest of us must guess how he's feeling— whether he's happy or mad, cross or sleepy.

I've put a small chair and a large chair together, so that you can step from the floor to the seat of the small chair and from the small chair to the large. Standing on the floor, say "one" in a low voice; step to the seat of the little chair and say "two" in a somewhat higher voice; and finally, step to the big chair and say "three" in a very high voice. If you succeed in making each step sound higher, the rest of us will clap the number of times you've said—1, 2, or 3.

Tom brought a toy roller coaster to school today and we're going to turn it into a sound coaster for our speech class. We'll take each vowel separately and make it go up and down as the car on the roller coaster climbs up and roars down the track. Let's take *ah* first. . . . Here, I will wind up the little car. . . . You must watch it carefully so that you can make your voice rise and fall as the car goes up and down on the roller coaster.

## NOT HIGH, BUT WIDE AND HANDSOME

"Speak up!" or "Louder, please" often produces not only an increase in volume but a rise in pitch as well. The result may be a shrill voice that pains the listener's ear and the speaker's throat. Adults are as guilty of this as children—perhaps more so, since they often feel required to make themselves heard. Children suffer under no such compulsion, unless their teacher requires that they put forth an effort to make themselves heard. Almost unconsciously, however, everyone prolongs the vowels when trying to project his voice. Mothers calling for their children produce quite a sustained vowel tone, especially if their children are in the next block. This is often accompanied by an unbecoming shriek as they call and call without an audible or visible response from their offspring. Children, too, tend to strain when attempting to project their voices. They have not learned to make the fullest use of the resonating cavities of the throat or to prolong the vowels. To help them learn "to project with polish," there are several activities which might help:

This rolled-up newspaper will be our megaphone. First, I want you to listen to how I sound when I speak through the megaphone. I'm not going to raise my voice as I speak through it. Listen hard and tell me if my voice seems louder or softer. "Recess will be at two-thirty today.". . . Was my voice any different? Yes, it sounded louder, didn't it? That's because I used the megaphone to help me; but I can do the same thing without it, because I have a megaphone inside my mouth as well. We all do! We have cavities in the back of our mouths that catch the sound and can make it louder. Let's see if we can use an outside megaphone—then the inside one. Cup your hands around your mouth and say, "Christmas vacation is coming." . . . Good. Now make your voice sound exactly the same way, only use the megaphone inside your throat and mouth.

I'd like each of you to imitate your father or mother calling you when you are far away from the house. Go into the cloakroom and call from there. The rest of us will listen and will write down the part of your name we hear most clearly and the sound which we hear the longest. Lynn, will you be first? (Teacher helps children recognize and write down vowels as they are prolonged.)

I've given red and green cards to the five people at the beginning of each row. They are going to be our judges. Everyone is going to have a chance to tell all of us the game he likes to play best. There's one catch—he must go to the back of the room, and he must make everyone in the room hear without raising his voice to a higher pitch. If his voice begins to go up, the judges will raise their red cards. As soon as the voice is loud, but not high, they'll put up their green cards.

### TONAL TECHNIQUES

There is a great variation in the characteristic tonal quality of voices, but even in adults the tonal quality of the average voice can hardly be said to be exhilarating. When we stop to realize that others pay as much attention to *how* we say something as to *what* we say, and sometimes more, a pleasant voice becomes a pertinent point. Children react to the tone of voice as well as to the words spoken. They are sensitive to the emotions betrayed through tonal quality. Even more, they need to develop their own tonal patterns.

Teachers can help children develop a tonal quality that is pleasant to the listener's ears. No stereotyped pattern should be set up, however; each child will have his own personal and characteristic tonal quality which is part of his personality.

We're going to play a matching game today. We will match our voices to some records I have here. First, I'm going to play a march. Listen, and then I'll take off the record and we'll count in march time, making our voices sound like the music. Good. . . . Now here's a waltz. Say, "Like to swing, like to sway," when I stop the record. Make sure your voice sounds like the music. Here's a record about rain falling. . . . Listen, and then we'll say "Pitter-patter," trying to use the same kind of sound we hear in the record.

I've drawn a big hill on the blackboard . . . and here's a little boy on a sled. As he goes sliding down the hill, our voices will slide down, too. Let's start with some of the vowels, and then we'll use some words.

You remember when the sixth-grade orchestra came in last week and showed us how they played their instruments. Today we'll have our own orchestra, using our voices instead of musical instruments. We'll choose violins and clarinets and a drum and a piano, and some others. For example, the violins will have a different tone from the tone of the drums or the bass fiddle. We'll choose the orchestra by closing our eyes and listening to each person.

I'd like to have you write down on a slip of paper the name of the grownup you think has the nicest voice. We'll put all the slips in a box and draw them out one at a time. Then you imitate the voice of the person you wrote down, and the rest of the class will try to guess who it is.

# IX

## *Speech as a Safety Valve of the Emotions*

WE MUST remember that speech has other functions besides communication and thinking. One of the most important of its uses is an outlet for the emotions. Perhaps more of our actual talking is spent in expressing our attitudes and feelings than for any other purpose. Sometimes we want other people to know when we are happy or hurt or angry but often the sheer verbal expression is all we need. Speech is very necessary to the satisfying experience of "blowing one's top." A temper tantrum on the floor is much less becoming for an adult. Words can hurt as much as blows. The bath of self-pity in which we anoint our wounded egos is usually a bath of words, spoken either aloud or silently. It is a sad sack of a person who must suffer silently all the time. Speech can be a wonderful safety valve when the pressure of emotion threatens to burst the rivets of our self-control.

Yet there are too many of us who never learn to use our speech in this way. Perhaps we had parents who kept things to themselves, who repressed all vocal expression of emotion, who buried the worry or the fear or the anger too deeply for words. These individuals have not learned to talk themselves out of the tangles of their frustrations. As every psychiatrist knows, there is need for verbal catharsis in all of us. When we can talk about the troubles that beset us, we often discover not only the fine calmness which follows such verbal release but, more important still, solutions for the problems which had previously seemed insoluble.

## TALKING IT OUT

Most of us have learned to prize a confidant we can trust, someone to whom we can tell our troubles. As we talk, we first experience relief and then begin to see the faint traces of a path out of the deep woods of our dank emotion. Our words are footsteps. As a few landmarks appear, no longer are we helpless and lost. Often we hardly hear the good advice of our confidant, so intent are we in following the faint trail which seems somehow to lead us out of the wilderness. We need our confidant's ear much more than we need his mouth. What his presence gives us is the necessity to keep talking sense. His questions often hinder more than help, but if we can see ourselves reflected in his responses we find the image truly healing. Speech is a powerful medicine for the sick of soul.

All of us must sooner or later suffer emotionally in this tough world of ours. The need to belong, the need for status, the need to protect what we have, the need to win more— all these are characteristic of the culture in which we spend our lives. So fierce is the competition that all of us will know hurt, failure, and frustration. Is there no place in the curriculum for teaching our children how to meet these crises? Every good teacher does what she can to protect and to soothe the child who finds himself entangled in the meshes

**Talk It Out! Don't Blow Your Top!**

of his misfortunes. But we should teach our children how to handle their troubles themselves. They will not always have someone near to support the shaky ego, to give aid and comfort. Specifically, we feel that children should be trained in the use of speech as a mental medicine. This is not to imply that we need make psychiatrists or psychiatric cases of our pupils, but merely to suggest that they get some permissive experience in expressing their emotions through speech and in the verbal solving of emotional problems. We teach the use of a toothbrush and oral hygiene. Surely it is as important to teach the principles of speech hygiene.

**CATHARSIS**

How can this be done? We have found that one of the best methods involves the dynamics of identification. Children are much more adept than adults in identifying. They can throw themselves wholeheartedly and without self-consciousness into many roles. They empathize easily. What the teacher does, therefore, is to create some character in troubles of various sorts, and then to help the children tell how the character is feeling and what he is thinking. Fist puppets, acting out a conflict situation, a story of an unhappy girl, an anecdote about a bully, a fairy tale of misfortune, a recorded playlet, a film, an actual testimonial from one of the children—any of these can serve as the basic problem to be presented. The teacher then begins to verbalize her guess as to how the characters are feeling, almost in a kind of self-talk or running commentary. Always the children chime in, adding, contradicting, supplementing from their own similar experiences, and getting a great amount of direct or vicarious catharsis from the process.

## PROBLEM SOLVING

But speech hygiene is more than mere catharsis. It involves problem solving, too. By presenting a story or a miniature playlet or puppet drama and stopping it abruptly, we provide the opportunity for emotional problem solving to occur. The children want to finish the story and they usually want it to turn out happily, so, with the teacher's help, they begin to suggest various endings. We often end the speech improvement period with an unfinished playlet or story of this sort and tell the children that we will finish it when speech improvement time comes around again. Then at the beginning of the subsequent period we ask them if they have been able to figure out what did happen. It is surprising to most teachers to see the wealth of suggestions and the high interest shown. Children hunger for experiences of this type. They want to know how the little boy learned to stop crying whenever he made a mistake in spelling. They find Oscar-the-puppet most intriguing when he makes the playground bully stop pushing him around. The story of the boy who never played with the other kids until one day he . . . always sets their imaginations to working overtime. And so, by presenting the gamut of frustrations, failures, rejections, and all the other unpleasant problems of daily living together, with the need to find solutions, we help children learn to handle their emotional lives.

Here are some specific suggestions to the elementary teacher:

1. Have a puppet named Oscar who is always getting into trouble and telling the class about it. "What shall we do with Oscar?" Reverbalize what the children offer and then

let Oscar respond, expressing his feelings so they can understand how such a person feels. If he gets too "ornery," the children can say, "Back in your box."

2. Have a go-to-bed scene all full of trouble, anger, and upset feelings. Have another go-to-bed scene which is good. Tell the children about both scenes and then act them out. Then ask the children what the first child would dream about in a "tell-your-neighbor" activity. Ask them what the second child would dream about. The teacher could change this by telling the dreams and asking which child had them.

3. The teacher can act out (by standing tall for the adult role and crouching down for the child) scenes of discipline, unreasonable demands, teacher-child relations, etc. After acting out part of a scene, ask the children what to say next.

4. Act out and verbalize three roles: the bully, the cry-baby, the well-adjusted child. Name each and put on a different cap or clothing until the children know one from another. Then place the caps or clothing on the desk. Act out a new role situation, asking them to identify you by the cap. Then tell why you got that way, and tell the children how you are going to change. Show them that Mr. Hyde can become Dr. Jekyll by shifting from one role to another.

5. Act out and verbalize the child's version of the Poor Soul, the neglected one, the last one chosen, and how he found a friend and soon became the "life of the party." Many children remain in their roles merely because they never realize they can change and become adequate.

6. Act out various reactions to failure and ask the children to tell which is best. Do the same for frustration, worry, guilt, etc.
7. Help the children daydream. Do some daydreaming aloud; then have them all do some themselves.

# X

## *Helping Children with Speech Defects in the Classroom*

🦋 MANY a classroom teacher would like to help a child who has a speech difficulty, but feels that she might do some unknown harm while trying to correct the child's speech. Speech defects seem mysterious at first. Why can't the child talk the way the others do? What's wrong? The teacher is often afraid to tamper with the unknown. Then, too, there is something mysterious about the manner in which the child vanishes from the classroom for "speech," if the school system employs a speech correctionist. All too often, the activities carried on by the speech correctionist are little understood by classroom teachers. This is how they feel:

Well, to tell you the truth, I never knew what the correctionist did with Jimmy. He went out of the room twice a week for a half-hour of speech, but I never heard about what he did during the time. Finally, at the end of the year I got a report for his cumulative record. By that time, it was too late for *me* to help him.

A kindergarten teacher chimed in:

I've never had a course in speech correction, and I'm afraid to tackle the job in the classroom. What if I did the wrong thing? Yet I'd like to help if I only knew how!

A first-grade teacher pointed out:

It isn't as though I haven't tried to help. Whenever I hear Mary make a mistake, I stop her and have her try to say the word over again. I've become very discouraged, though. Most of the time, she'll just say it the same old way and I don't seem to be making any progress at all. Why does she have to keep on saying it the wrong way when I've just told her the correct way?

## CHILDREN WITH DEFECTIVE SPEECH

There are three main types of speech defects: defects of *articulation*, of *rhythm*, and of *voice*. For the most part, the classroom teacher will have contact with the first two. As a matter of fact, the great majority of children with defective speech will exhibit *articulation* (or pronunciation) errors. Over two-thirds of the speech-defective children the teacher encounters will have an articulation defect. For one reason or another, they just cannot say the speech sounds the way the normal-speaking child does. Second in point of frequency are the rhythm disorders, the most important of these being *stuttering*. Stuttering is characterized by broken, nonfluent speech. Another name for the same disorder is *stammering*. Few voice disorders, except an occasional cleft-palate child, are seen by the classroom teacher.

## HELPING A CHILD WITH AN ARTICULATION DEFECT

Fortunately, the teacher can be of the greatest assistance to those children who compose the great bulk of the speech-defective group, the children who exhibit an articulation defect. She need not fear that she will do the "wrong thing" if she follows the suggestions in the preceding chapters. She will find that children who have a mild articulation defect, with only a few errors, will respond readily to the speech improvement program which has been outlined, and may need little or no additional help.

Children whose articulation errors are more frequent and severe will still benefit greatly from the speech improvement program. It can be used as the basis for additional individual work.

Before starting individual work, the teacher must locate exactly the sounds which are being omitted, distorted, or substituted. She will find as she listens to the child's speech (in reading, for example) that there are some sounds which he habitually mispronounces. The sounds which are usually defective are those which were emphasized in Chapter IV, "The Alphabet of Sound."

What does the teacher listen for? First, she listens for:

*Sound substitutions and distortions:*

S (lisping). The child substitutes some other sound for the *sss* sound. There are several kinds of lisps, but they all involve a distortion of the *sss* or a substitution of another sound for the *sss*. Soap becomes *tho*ap or *to*ap or *sho*ap.

Sh, ch. These two sounds are sometimes confused. *Ch*icken becomes *sh*icken; while *sh*oe becomes *ch*oe.

L. Most commonly, *w* is substituted for *l*. A *l*ittle *l*amp becomes a *w*ittle *w*amp.

Th. The child often substitutes another sound for the *th*— most commonly an *f* or an *s*. *Th*umb becomes *f*um; too*th* may be too*s*.

R. When the *r* is defective at the beginning of a word, it will sound like a *w*; *r*abbit becomes *w*abbit. When the *r* is defective in the middle or at the end of words, it is usually some *distortion* of the *errrr* sound.

*Sound omissions and additions:* The teacher will rarely encounter a sound addition (brrlue for blue) but will often find children omitting some of their speech sounds. The blends, such as *sl, bl, br,* are especially difficult for early elementary children. Many a child goes to "kool," not *sc*hool, because of the difficulty in using an *s* blend. The *s,* a sound which has a high frequency and may not be noted by the unobservant ear, seems to be omitted more frequently than the others. At times it is omitted in the middle and at the end of words as well as in the beginning.

In listening for these sound substitutions, distortions, omissions, and additions, the teacher is acting as her own troubleshooter. She must locate the sounds which are difficult for the child. After she has found them, she is ready to help him. It is now his turn to listen.

What does the child listen for? First of all, he listens to the teacher making the various speech sounds. He listens for his "good" sound. He must be able to *hear* the difference between his error and the correct sound. In the beginning, identification of sounds and discrimination between the good and the bad sound are done by the teacher. We must sharpen the child's ears. The child is only required to *listen* and to indicate his judgment.

It is only after several such sessions of "ear training" that the teacher asks the child to *make* the sound. Even then, she asks him to make the sound in isolation only. He attempts to utter the speech sound all alone, all by itself. Why? Because if the child is now told, "Jimmy, say 'sister,'" he will in all likelihood respond with "thithter." All his past experience with the *s* sound has been in using that sound as if it were *th.* He has used the error in that word too many times. A new, correct sound is too weak to win out against such competition. Therefore, the child is asked only to utter a new and different sound. It may seem wrong to him at first and certainly it will be unfamiliar. The teacher attempts to break down the old habits by first teaching this sound alone; then, when it is strong enough, she very slowly integrates it into the child's speech. Any attempt to rush the new sound into words will result in the emergence again of the defective sound.

Let us describe the sequence again up to this point. First, we do some ear training. Then, we teach the sound in isolation. Next, the sound is strengthened so that it will be able to stand and compete with the defective sound.

We strengthen the new sound also in combination with other speech sounds. Call it what you will—"babbling," "monkey talk," "sound sandwiches," "nonsense syllables"— the focal point of this step is having the child use his new sound, not in isolation, but with all of the vowel sounds. For example, in a "sound sandwich," he uses his good sound as the filling in the sandwich, while the vowels are the slices of bread. An open-face sandwich is one like this: *oos, ahs, ees, os;* or *see, sai, soo, so, say.* Close the sandwich and the new sound is neatly cushioned between two vowels: *eesee, oosoo, ahsah, oso, aisai.* When the child can use his "good sound," combined with these vowels, with speed and precision, he is ready to put that new sound into words.

In this final step the teacher helps the child put his good sound into words and, eventually, the words into sentences. Even at this stage of the game the teacher cannot expect the child suddenly to start saying all the familiar *s* words correctly. As in the beginning of the therapy, she must make haste slowly. She can help the child work on only a few words at a time so that he gradually accumulates a great many words which have the new, good sound firmly implanted. Once the sound is safely grafted into words, it starts its growth in the sentence structure.

It is a great temptation to work on more than one sound when a child has several which are defective. This is likely to be an almost fatal fascination. The child tends to be all the more confused if he must adjust to more than one new concept of speech sounds simultaneously. Only after one sound can be used habitually and unconsciously in several key words and the child can correct himself should he be encouraged to tackle another of his errors.

Now comes the question of which sound is to be chosen when there are several needing correction. The teacher first identifies all the defective sounds and then has the child attempt to make each sound in *isolation*. She then chooses the sound which is most accurately and easily reproduced. It is important that the child have some success right from the start. If the most difficult sound were chosen, both child and teacher would be likely to become discouraged. Success breeds further speech attempts; the child who succeeds in mastering one sound will be better equipped to handle another and more difficult sound.

So much of the phonic material used in the teaching of reading stresses speech sounds at the beginning of words only that it is often difficult to remember that these sounds appear in the middle and at the end of words as well. In helping a child use his good sound in words, it is well to use it at the beginning of words at first, and then to follow with words which have the sound in the other two positions as well.

Often the child experiences the least difficulty in using his new sound at the beginning of words, with more difficulty present in remembering to use it at the end of words and the most difficulty in using it in the middle of words where it is tucked away among other sounds. The words which the teacher may use for speech work should be selected with this in mind.

With this basic knowledge, the teacher can help any child with an articulation defect work on his speech, with an expenditure of five or ten minutes of her time each day. Her reward often will be an improvement in the child's speech which is beyond her expectations.

### CHILDREN WHO STUTTER

The stuttering child presents a much more difficult problem for the classroom teacher. If only for the purposes of self-defense, she should know enough about this disorder to protect her from parents who tend to put the blame upon the classroom teacher for any appearance of stuttering or increase in its severity. Few articulation cases get worse in school; many stutterers do. Teachers, with the best of intentions, have often adopted policies which result in more frequent and more severe blockings. So it is wise to learn about stuttering.

The first important bit of knowledge is that stuttering is a progressive disorder; it grows and changes its form. Beginning with simple repetitions or prolongations much like the non-fluency of the average child under communicative stress, it progresses through a transitional stage of struggle and contortion into the severe fear-infested variety called secondary stuttering.

There are a few basic facts. Stuttering occurs in at least one person in every hundred. There are at least four times as many boys as girls who stutter. Stuttering usually begins in the preschool period and gets worse in the early elementary and much worse in the high-school years. Children in the first stage (hereafter called the primary stuttering stage) often seem to overcome it without much help and usually before the age of ten. Those who struggle with their words and show facial contortions are in much greater danger but may still regress through primary stuttering into normal speech. They are said to have transitional stuttering. They need help. Children who, in their struggle, add fears of sounds, words, or speech situations are said to have secondary stuttering, the chronic form which seldom disappears without intensive and expert therapy.

### PRIMARY STUTTERING

The primary stutterer shows his difficulty in repetitions and prolongations of sounds and syllables. All children have some of these when under stress as well as many other types of hesitation or repetition of words or phrases. We become concerned only when there are too many repetitions of sounds or syllables per word and too many words upon which repetitions occur. How many is too many? All we can say is that when speech becomes noticeably impaired, when communication becomes difficult, when there is so much of this repeating that the child or his classmates will sooner or later come to recognize it as abnormal, a diagnosis of stuttering should be made. A few repetitions should be ignored. But when we find many of them, occurring too frequently under conditions where there is little or no apparent excitement or emotion, we should begin to be concerned. It is wise to make the diagnosis of stuttering with caution, but we must not fail to recognize that the more severe varieties of stuttering start with these same symptoms.

Once you are pretty well convinced that this syllable and sound repetition or prolongation is no temporary bit of behavior, you should attempt to discover what types of pressures make it appear. Usually hurry, excitement, the loss of a listener, competition, the need to communicate unpleasant information, the necessity for formulating and expressing complicated thoughts, the fear of rejection, and many similar disturbing influences will increase the child's difficulty. Your job is to remove or reduce these pressures. Once you recognize them, you will find a way.

The primary stutterer often has periods of complete fluency for days or even weeks at a time. Take advantage of these fluent periods and encourage the child to talk as much as possible. When he is having some of his nonfluent days, it is wise to arrange things so he has less need to talk. This policy alone has freed many such children.

We do not call the child's attention to his primary stuttering in any way. We try to keep him completely unaware that anything abnormal is occurring. We do not help him with his difficult words; we merely wait calmly and casually until he has finished. We do not ask him to stop and start over, to take a new breath, to relax, to think what he is trying to say. All such requests merely help him to become conscious of his impediment and will tend to make it worse. The child himself seems completely unaware that any nonfluency is occurring. He just babbles away. If we can keep him from becoming frustrated or building up fear of speaking, nature will usually take care of the problem and he will become fluent again. Indirect treatment is the wisest course to follow.

Primary stutterers should not be given opportunities to display their speech in school programs, recitations before strangers, or other similar activities because a single unfortunate experience in which they find themselves frustrated or mocked may change the disorder from simple automatic repetitions into profound struggle and contortion. On the other hand, such a child should not be made to feel different by excusing him from all verbal participation in school. He should have his regular turn, but the amount of speech required should be brief and he should be called upon to say things that he knows and things that can be expressed fairly simply.

Many children go through a period of primary stuttering when they are beset by conflicts that they cannot solve. Some of these may be in the home and perhaps a talk with one of the parents may help. But there are other conflicts occurring in school or on the playground which the classroom teacher can do much to reduce or eliminate. A child living in fear that when he goes home from school he must run a cruel gauntlet of teasing, bullying, or cruelty will not be a fluent child. The stutterer may need a little extra love or attention and not much else to allow him to speak easily rather than hesitantly.

Children who live in insecurity show it in their speech. Help such children to gain self-respect and confidence. Give them opportunities to shine, to feel worthy. A little responsibility and appreciation works wonders. It is not much to give and often it is enough. Often with primary stutterers we need only remove the straw from the camel's back; we need remove but one single pressure, or add but one little bit to the child's ego, and the nonfluency disappears.

## TRANSITIONAL STUTTERING

We need not worry too much about the primary stutterer. Often, in spite of unfavorable home environment or pronounced emotional conflicts he finds a path out of his difficulties. But there are some primary stutterers who do become conscious of their repeating and prolonging. Parents, classmates, or teachers, well-meaning enough but ignorant of the nature of the disorder, "correct" the child and make him become unpleasantly aware of his broken speech. At first this awareness is only intermittent; he soon forgets all about it. Later on, if it is brought to his attention often enough, he does begin to hear it and feel it. At this point he tries to do something. The repetitions become faster; forcing and tension appear. He begins to struggle to release himself from the repetitions and prolongations which interrupt his communication. This is the picture of "transitional stuttering." The more he struggles, the worse he becomes blocked, for he struggles randomly. Facial contortions begin to appear, with head jerks and body movements reflecting the spreading tension. Small tremors or vibrations are seen in the lips, jaw, or tongue. The child still makes an attempt to talk as he always did, but he experiences great difficulty in communicating. Often at this time he will show changes in personality, depressions or bursts of hostility and anxiety. He may become a behavior problem. He does not avoid speaking situations or certain words; he seems to have no fear of talking. But his stuttering frustrates him terribly. As in primary stuttering, the blocks come in waves; he will have good days and bad days. When things are going well, he may be symptom-free for weeks at a time. During his bad periods he may find himself almost helpless so far as communication is concerned.

The classroom teacher must view her role with the transitional stutterer as a supportive, protective one. The treatment must generally follow the same principles as that governing the primary stutterer, because in many cases the child still has an excellent chance to return to the primary stage. This is hard for most teachers to realize when the contortions and struggle are so evident. But little children swiftly forget their discomfort. The important thing is to prevent the child from reacting to his stuttering by avoiding speaking. Without his realizing it, classes must be so handled as to keep him from having his speech difficulty exposed for himself and others to see. When he does speak, he must be made to feel that there is no hurry, no impatience, that he has all the time in the world to utter what he is trying so hard to say. Be sure to look at him calmly. Do not help him with his words. Refuse to let the other children interrupt him. Do not ask him to stop, to relax, to think what he is going to say. Just show, by your own behavior, that you too have plenty of time and that you are not distressed. Occasionally, restate what he has said, after he has finished, in such a manner that he almost feels that he has said it himself. This will show him that he has communicated and it will leave him with the impression of fluency rather than the memory of horrible struggle. Create opportunities for class recitation in unison so that he can feel fluent, for he will speak well under this condition.

If he stutters so hard that he gives up or begins to cry or

comes to you for help after class, have a little talk with him. Tell him that many children go through a period of trying too hard when they talk and that it will soon pass away, especially if he takes it easy. Give him reassurance that this is a temporary condition. Point out the times when he has been fluent and tell him you'll call on him for the things he knows and give him plenty of time.

If other children notice it or begin to tease, protect him. Just point out casually that you get all tangled up in expressing yourself sometimes too and so do they. Occasionally call attention in a good-natured manner to some of the non-fluency which they also show. If some little ringleader takes it upon himself to bedevil the stutterer, call the former aside and explain that his actions may make the stutterer worse. Then ask him to keep the other children from teasing or mockery.

Many transitional stutterers are able to read without difficulty or can recite memorized passages with ease. Others can speak well when they are in command. Create situations of this sort so that some nucleus of fluent speech is experienced each day. As in primary stuttering, take advantage of the good periods to evoke much speech, and reduce the amount of communication necessary on his bad days. Do not free him from all recitation or participation under any circumstances. Help him to feel that he is an important member of the group. Build his ego and self-confidence in every way available.

Some of these children are having troubles at home or on the playground. Try to locate these and do what you can to decrease them. A parent conference often helps, especially if the parents are doing all the wrong things. Sometimes these children regain their fluency almost immediately if they can just have some kind, understanding person to tell their troubles to. Be that person. Help them to release their emotion. Make them feel that at least someone understands, respects, and is fond of them.

## SECONDARY STUTTERING

Secondary stuttering is the advanced stage of the disorder. It is marked by all the symptoms of primary and transitional stuttering, but, in addition, the child has learned to fear sounds, words, and situations. This fear causes more stuttering. A vicious cycle has been started and the child begins to use avoidances of all kinds. He may refuse to talk, use synonyms for his hard words, postpone the speech attempt or employ various gestures, "ahs," and "ums" to get started. You will see many tremors (vibrations) of the lips, jaw, or tongue. Occasionally the child will open his mouth and nothing will come forth despite strong struggle. Often, at this stage, peculiar habits of mouth posturing, jaw jerks, eye blinks, lip protrusions become fixed parts of the stuttering. The child feels quite helpless, unable to speak, caught between the twin urges to talk and not to talk. He knows only too well that he stutters.

These children should be referred to a speech therapist, speech clinic, or child guidance clinic for study. Ask the therapist to give you a summary of the findings and a set of recommendations. Most secondary stutterers need expert help, more than you can give. But since you still have them in your classes, it is wise to have a definite policy to follow. We suggest that, in general, you carry out much the same procedures that we have outlined for the transitional stutterer, but with one major difference. You should have a talk with the child, telling him that you are aware of his stuttering and wish to help. Tell him that you know how difficult it is for him to talk easily and that you will call on him for short recitations only, but that if he will raise his hand, you will always give him a chance to talk no matter how much he stutters. Help him to see that avoiding speech only makes the stuttering worse in the long run. And get across to him this one important point: that it is possible to stutter in many ways, and that some forms are much better than others. Tell him that he must learn to stutter easily, effortlessly, and without contortion, that he must learn *to stutter slowly and smoothly*. Do some practice with him after school, rehearsing the answers to questions you may ask him the following day. Help him to see that he can touch stuttering without panic, that if he will just try to work out of his blockings smoothly the words will come out much quicker. Praise him for "good stuttering" rather than for fluent speech, since the more you reward the latter, the more painful will the stuttering become. Help him to accept the fact that he has this problem and must learn to live with it as comfortably as possible until he can receive the intensive speech therapy which is required. Get him to verbalize his fears, his aching memories of blocking in important situations. Protect him from penalty and give him none yourself. Just one person who understands is a tremendous help to the child with a twisted tongue. Be that person!

# Appendix

Appendix

# *Typical Speech Improvement Lesson Plans*

## KINDERGARTEN

(This particular plan was used after twelve half-hour sessions in the kindergarten.)

1. **ALPHABET OF SOUNDS**            Game: *Silent Sounds*

    Material: Pictures of the 8 sounds (*r, s, l, ch, sh, k, f, th*). These pictures are personifications of the sounds—*r* is a red fire engine, etc.

    Instructions: Review sounds with child placing cards along chalk rail of blackboard. Then have children lip-read sounds. For example, form *sh* silently with your lips, then choose some child to pick out right picture. That child says sound out loud to class, and they repeat. Another child is chosen for next sound, etc.

2. **VOCAL PHONICS**        Game: *What Are You Wearing?*

    Material: None

    Instructions: Sound out various articles of apparel—sock, shoes, sweater, shirt, skirt, etc. Have children point. Vary this by saying, "All the girls point to a boy wearing a *sss–w–ea–t–er*." "All the boys point to a girl who is wearing a *ss–k–ir–t*."

165

"Everyone point to someone who's wearing the color *rrr–e–d*."

3. DISCRIMINATION (between *sh* and *ch*)        Game: *Asleep or Awake*

Material: None

Instructions: All children stand. Every time they hear the *sh* sound, they pretend to go to sleep—lay their heads on their hands. When they hear the train sound, they are wide awake, and jump *once*. Alternate sounds. Start with isolated sounds, then say nonsense syllables and finally words.

4. TONGUE EXERCISE                Game: *Let's Be a Circus*

Material: None

Instructions: "Let's pretend our tongues are going to a circus. First, let's hop on to the merry-go-round (tongue makes circle inside and outside mouth). Now have it be the pole that holds up the circus tent (tongue up toward nose). Now it's a man on a trapeze (swing from side to side). See the horses go around the ring (tongues click like horses' hoofs). How fast can you make your horse go?" Etc.

5. PITCH                Game: *On a Roller Coaster*

Material: None

Instructions: "You've all seen a roller coaster, where the little cars go up and down like this (demonstrate with hand). Our right hands will be a roller coaster car, and we'll carry a sound up and down. Let's start with *oh*. Here we go, make the sound go up and down with our hand." (Go through other vowels.)

## FIRST GRADE

(This plan was used at almost the beginning of speech improvement lessons.)

1. ALPHABET OF SOUNDS        Game: *Balance the Sound*
   Material: Pictures of 8 sounds, as described in kindergarten lesson
   Instructions: Children identify all 8 sounds, then guess sound teacher is holding in her hand. One who gets it right walks across the room, balancing card on head. While he walks, all the rest of the children must make the sound he's carrying on his head. If it drops off, children stop making sound the minute it hits the floor.

2. INTENSITY        Game: *Growing Up*
   Material: None
   Instructions: Children squat on haunches and say in whisper, "I'm a little baby," then rise to halfway position, saying, "I'm a big girl (or boy)," then stand on tiptoes and shout, "I'm a giant."

3. FLUENCY        Game: *Fill-in Story*
   Material: None
   Instructions: Teacher explains that sometimes she can't find the word she's hunting for and she'd like to have the children help by filling in the words, when she gets stuck. Tells a story of the little boy who was late for school because he climbed a high fence and tore a hole in his pants. "Once upon a _____, there was a little boy who was always late for _____. He could never seem to get started on _____. His mother was always telling him to _____, but he was so _____. She always had his clothes laid out on the _____, but this one morning, she _____. So the little _____ grabbed his best pair of Sunday _____ and ran off to _____. He decided to take a short cut. He went across the field and climbed a high _____. And what

do you know? He tore a great big _____ right in the seat of his _____. He knew his mother would be very _____.

But he didn't want to go to school with that big _____ in the seat of his pants. So he started back for _____. When he got there and his mother saw what had happened to his best pair of _____, she said to him: _____ (have children verbalize what their mothers say). Yes, she said something like that. Then she made him put on a very old pair of blue _____ and go back to school. By this time, he was very late. When he finally reached _____, his teacher was very _____. And the little boy said to himself, "My goodness, grown-ups are *always* getting mad. I'm glad I'm just in first grade, and not grown up yet!"

4. VOCAL PHONICS                 Game: *Action Phonics*
    Material: None
    Instructions: "You know, sometimes I stretch out words like a rubber band until they break in their several parts. Today when I stretch the word out of shape out loud, and you put it back into shape in your mind, I want you to *do* as I say, rather than to point. Let's see if you can all *ssss–t–a–nd*. Good. Now let's *j–u–m–p*." (Do others—wave, smile, hop, skip, run, turn, etc. End with *sss–i–t*.)

5. CORRECTION OF SOUNDS        Game: *Help the Puppet*
    Material: Hand Puppet
    Instructions: Children point to various things in the room, and the puppet tries to say them. Children tell him if he's right or wrong by telling him to put his hands over his ears if he's wrong, and clap his hands if he's right.

## SECOND GRADE

(This plan was used after five sessions.)

1. ALPHABET OF SOUNDS             Game: *Quick Sit*

    Material: None

    Instructions: Teacher introduces game with quick review of 8 sounds. Then the room is divided into three or four sections, each section assigned a sound. Everyone stands. Children must sit down quickly when teacher says their particular sound. After a few run-throughs, choose different children to be the teacher. (I don't know why they get such a bang out of this one, but they certainly like it!)

2. VOCAL PHONICS              Game: *Shut-Eye TV*

    Material: None

    Instructions: All the children close their eyes and listen while teacher sounds out the names of different personalities they watch on TV. The moment they know who it is, they open their eyes, then click on TV (turn "knob" with fingers) and answer in unison. Sound out such things as Lassie, Superman, Space Cadets, Rin-Tin-Tin, etc.

3. SPEECH HYGIENE              Game: *He Won't*

    Material: Puppet

    Instructions: The puppet has visited the class previously and always been fluent if not correct. This time, after trying and failing once or twice, he refuses to talk. He won't talk, he won't look at anyone, he won't do anything; so the teacher asks for help from the children. How can they help him want to talk again? It's amazing, the kind of responses that this problem brings out. Choose the best solution offered and try to work it out. If none are applicable, say, "Well, perhaps if you all talk together in an *echo* game, he'll talk, too."

4.  PITCH AND INTENSITY                    Game: *Be My Echo*
        Material: None
        Instructions: "Be sure to say exactly what I say, in exactly the way I say it. (Whisper) I like to wiggle. (Loud) I want to play." (Etc. Combine various pitch levels, inflections, and intensity levels with mental hygiene material.)

## THIRD GRADE

1.  ALPHABET OF SOUNDS                    Game: *Circling Sounds*
        Material: Volleyball or small softball
        Instructions: Children form a circle; sounds are reviewed. Then ball is tossed haphazardly from one child to another. Each succeeding child must produce a different sound in isolation. If he repeats sound said by the person just before him, he is out of the game. Sound must be produced at the same instant the ball is caught.

2.  VOICE PRODUCTION                    Game: *Be an Actor*
        Material: None
        Instructions: Unison speech activity. Teacher gives each sentence, children repeat. "I feel cross today." "I am so sleepy." "I can hardly wait for Christmas." "I wish I didn't have to go to school." "I feel happy inside." Demonstrate voice qualities—cross, tired, excited, etc.

3.  VOCAL PHONICS                    Game: *Shoot the Soldier*
        Material: None
        Instructions: This is a variation of Phonics Up Front (where children help teacher sound out word). Teacher introduces three or four speech sounds

again (ex.: *r, s, l,* and *th*), then has two
children come up, one on either side of her.
She whispers a sound in their ear, and when
she taps them, they say their sound. First
child says "*m*," teacher (in the middle) says
"*ou*," and child on other side says "*th*." The
children are supposed to shoot (with their
finger) the person up front who makes one of
the four sounds introduced. Other children
are chosen to help sound out other words
(such as run, soap, look). Teacher usually
takes vowel, but can be "shot" by taking position at either end.

4. TONGUE COÖRDINATION                Game: *Lion Hunt*
   Material: None
   Instructions: Tongue exercise to go with story: "A little
   boy went with his father to hunt lions in the
   jungle. The first morning he decided to run
   away and hunt for a lion by himself. So while
   everyone was sleeping, he ran away into the
   jungle (make tongue move in and out rapidly). But he soon got tired (tongue moves
   more and more slowly), until he stopped—
   but he couldn't see any lions. He decided to
   climb a tree (tongue toward nose) to take a
   better look around (tongue makes circle outside of mouth). When he got to the top of
   the tree he looked down (point tongue toward
   chin) and saw a river. Now this smart little
   boy knew that all animals had to have water
   to drink (tongue laps up water) and so he slid
   down the tree (tongue moves swiftly from up
   toward nose, down toward chin) and ran to
   the river. And sure enough, there was a lion
   drinking. So the little boy raised his gun and
   fired twice (two tongue clicks). The lion fell

over (tongue falls from ridge behind upper teeth as in saying *la*). The little boy picked up the dead lion and tried to carry him, but he was awfully heavy, and the little boy looked like this . . . (tongue moves in and out, but way on one side of the mouth). Meanwhile, what do you think the daddy was doing? What would your daddy do if you'd run away and were lost in a jungle? Yes, he was out looking for the little boy. And when he found him, they carried the lion together—swinging it between them (tongue moves from side to side). And the little boy was so glad to see his daddy that he decided never to go lion hunting alone again."

5. **General Speech Improvement**    Game: *Teacher Makes a Mistake*

   Material: None

   Instructions: "I'm going to be a third-grader now and show you different ways of talking." (Act out and have children tell you your mistake—talking with hands in mouth, in a monotone, too fast, too loud, too soft, etc.)

## FOURTH GRADE

1. **Alphabet of Sound**    Game: *Buzz*

   Material: None

   Instructions: After reviewing alphabet of sounds, each row is assigned a sound. Children count off—one, two, three, etc. Children whose sound occurs in the number they must say, say "Buzz" instead. If they forget, they are out of the game. For example, the first row is given the *th* sound, the second row the *r* sound. First person in first row says "One," second person says "Two," third person must say "Buzz" instead of *th*ree. Have all children stand and, as they forget to say "Buzz," sit down. See how long they can remain standing.

2. VOCAL PHONICS                    Game: *Sports Parade*
   Material: None
   Instructions: Teacher says, "I'm going to sound out some sports—some games or activities. As soon as you guess what I've sounded out, raise your hand—the first one to guess comes up here to the front and can act it out for the rest of you." (Sound out skiing, swimming, wrestling, fighting, football, baseball, snowballing, etc.) Others then try to guess it.

3. FLUENCY STORY                    Game: *The Best Brother*
   Material: None
   Instructions: Have children "fill in." "Once upon a _____ there was a family who lived near here. There were two boys in the _____. At home, they got along together pretty well, but when they went to _____, they were always hitting and _____, yes, fighting. Bobby was in the fourth _____, and his brother, Jim, was in the third grade. Jim was good in all his _____, studies—he got A's in _____ and _____. Besides being good at school, he was good at throwing a _____ and everyone wanted him on their _____. Bobby, the one in _____ grade, had trouble with some of his studies, and he couldn't throw a _____ at all. Bobby couldn't seem to do anything as well as Jim, even if he was older. He got awful mad about it, too. At lunch, Bobby tried to help his _____ set the table. He reached for a bottle of milk, but it slipped and _____ to the floor. His mother said, "Now

look what you've _____. And I just finished scrubbing this _____! Why can't you be more _____? Honestly, you just can't do anything _____ right." Right then and there, Bobby decided he'd have to do something. He was sick and _____ of always getting jumped on and always making _____. What do you think he did? (Have children guess.) Well, next week, when I come back, I'll tell you what Bobby decided to do."

## FIFTH GRADE

1. ALPHABET OF SOUNDS       Game: *Find Your Brother*

    Material: Sound wheel (pie-shaped wheel divided in wedges with spinner in center; on wheel are voiced and unvoiced sounds—*k* and *g, s* and *z, t* and *d, th* and *th, b* and *p, f* and *v, sh* and *zh, ch* and *dj*, etc.)

    Instructions: Teacher spins pointer and sounds out letter at which it stops. Rest of the class must find its brother. Precede this by explanation of voiced and unvoiced sound—"made the same way, but one is noisy and one is quiet."

2. VOCAL PHONICS       Game: *Scrambled Phonics*

    Material: None

    Instructions: Since this was first time in the fifth grade, class did phonics forward; as an example: "*s–k–oo–l, t–ea–ch–er, N–o–v–em–ber*." Then came backward phonics: *t–s–i–r* (wrist), *k–oo–b* (book), etc. Then scrambled words were introduced—ones that make sense either way (loot, tool; tack, cat; mat, tam). Sound out and have them guess whether you're thinking of it forwards or backwards.

3. DISCRIMINATION                    Game: *Make Me Sit*
     Material: 2 chairs
     Instructions: "I have two chairs—one is a good speech
                        chair; this is the poor speech chair. I'm going
                        to try to fool you. I'll make some mistakes
                        while I'm talking. If you can catch me say,
                        *sit*—and I must sit in the poor speech chair.
                        I won't make my mistakes very noticeable—
                        you'll have to be quick to catch me. If I can
                        finish the sentence before you find my mis-
                        take, I'll sit down in the good speech chair."

4. VOICE                              Game: *Sound Alikes*
     Material: None
     Instructions: "During the next three minutes, I want each
                        of you to talk with as many others in the room
                        as you can. Your job is to find the person
                        whose voice sounds the most like yours.
                        You've heard about people who look alike but
                        are not twins; well, you won't find anyone
                        whose voice is just like yours, but you'll find
                        someone whose voice is more like yours than
                        anyone else's in the room. As soon as you've
                        found your 'sound alike,' come up to the front
                        of the room. Let's see how many pairs we can
                        get."

## SIXTH GRADE

1. VOCAL PHONICS             Game: *The Race to Planet X*
     Material: Felt board, 2 rocket ships, and planets—or
                  chalk and blackboard
     Instructions: If using felt board place rocket ships at oppo-
                        site corner at bottom of board. Put largest felt
                        circle (Planet X) at top, then scatter two or
                        three other planets (moon, etc.) between.
                        Divide class into two teams. Each team flies

one of the rockets. Sound out words like galaxy, jet, blast, space suit, Venus, Mars, Jupiter, ray gun, etc., giving each team alternate words. Each time someone on team guesses their rocket ship moves up another planet. First team to hit Planet X wins.

2. FLUENCY

Game: *Tall Tales*

Material: None

Instructions: "Today we'll have a Tall Tale time. We're going to be working on getting the 'ums' and 'uhs' and 'ahs' out of our talking. To do this, we're going to have Mary (first person in first row) start a story. It can be funny, or sad, or exciting—anything she pleases. But the first time she uses a 'staller' she has to sit down, and it will be the person behind her who has a chance. Since it's hard to know when you use a staller sometimes, the class is going to listen, and as soon as they hear one, we'll all shout, 'Down you go!' "

3. THINKING ALOUD

Game: *If I Were*

Material: None

Instructions: "I know you've all thought about what you'd like to do when you grow up—be a nurse, or a fireman, or a scientist, or a cowboy. Now close your eyes, and think about what you'd do if you were grown up and had the kind of job you want. When you feel a tap on your shoulder, stand up and start telling us, something like this: 'If I were a nurse, I'd take care of sick people. I want to go to a big city and be in the hospital.' You must stop talking when you hear my pencil hit the table. Then someone else will be tapped."

4. VOICE                                      Game: *Guess My Age*

    Material: None

    Instructions: "Everyone face the back of the room. I'm going to imitate several people I know. You are to guess the age of the person by the way my voice sounds. Perhaps you've never stopped to think about it, but you can often tell how old someone is by his voice. As I imitate the voices, I'm going to write their age on the blackboard. After I'm all done, you turn around and compare your guess with what I've written on the board." Imitate baby, sixth-grader, father, grandmother.

# Index